The Goddess Life

Inspiration & activities to align your mind, body & spirit

Cherise Williams

DEDICATION

This book is dedicated to the two most important Goddesses in my life.

To my mother Monica, thank you for your constant love and support of me. I truly don't know where I would be without you. I am the woman I am today because of you. You really are an angel on this earth.

To my daughter Makayla, you are my first true love. I never knew a love so eternally deep until I held you in my arms for the first time. You're an amazing person and I'm beyond thankful that I get to be your mother.

Words could never truly express how important you two are to me. I love you both dearly with every ounce of my being.

CONTENTS

ACKNOWLEDGMENTS

I'd like to acknowledge all of the amazing women that I've been blessed to have in my life. Especially all of the beautiful women in my family. You're amazing, strong and incredible. Each one of you have been such important people in my life. More than you may know.

To my cousin, Alicia Ritchey, thank you for the organizational help with this book, for your business insights, and for your friendship. So thankful we're cousins.

To my husband, Danny. I love you beyond words. Thank you for always standing by me and supporting my dreams, even when they didn't always make sense.

And to my beautiful son Dylan, my spiritual baby. You're a lovely ray of sunshine and your tender heart touches me. I love you so very much.

I would also like to acknowledge my friend Michelle Black. Thank you for your friendship and inspiring me to be a more gentle human.

Thank you to Nikki Hartley and Kaycee Bassett for your insights into this book and your constant encouragement of me.

Cory Gunn, thank you for your Goddess Guidance and for connecting me even more deeply to Athena. My business, and life, has truly benefited from it.

And to you, the beautiful goddess reading this book. Thank you for being here, in this time and in this space. Thank you for being you.

The Goddess Life

Following a short meditation one morning, the idea for this book popped into my head out of nowhere, like a bolt of lightning. Divine inspiration at its finest, and I immediately sat down to start writing. The format for the book changed slightly until it became what you're reading now. But it all seemed to flow so effortlessly. I've felt for a good few years that I was meant to write a book. But every time I tried to set out writing it, I would feel stuck. It always felt forced. So I would put it on the back burner until I would feel that familiar nudge again. But as I would attempt to write, that same forced feeling would rise up. However, once I opened myself up to divine guidance and stopped trying to force an outcome, this book was born.

I can see why I was divinely led to write this particular book. Within this book are things that I personally use every day within my own spiritual and holistic practice. They're things that helped me align my own body, mind and spirit. Things that helped me heal my relationship with myself, and helped me recognize and embrace my inner goddess.

I didn't always have such a good relationship with myself or Spirit. And don't get me wrong, it's still not always a cakewalk. But where I am currently, compared to where I used to be, is like night and day.

I used to hold a lot of shame, self-loathing, fear and anger within myself. I let life's circumstances bring me down. And life threw some pretty crappy stuff at me. As a child I experienced domestic violence and sexual abuse, two unrelated circumstances. As a teen and young adult it's no surprise that I would enter into a lot of relationships that weren't the best. Physical, sexual, emotional and mental abuse were common themes (until I met my husband). I tried to mask the pain and hide from myself by abusing drugs and alcohol. Which would then make me feel guilty, which made me feel more shame and self-loathing, so I would self-medicate again, look for love in all the wrong places…it was a vicious cycle to be in.

And through it all, I always kept a smile plastered to my face and never let anyone know what I was going through or feeling. Even those closest to me had no idea. I got so good at covering up my pain in front of others. But the pain and sadness were always there beneath the surface, and I felt so alone and lost.

As I got older and approached my thirties, I started to work on myself. To *truly* work on myself. I had quit drugs years prior after the birth of my beautiful daughter, but heavy social drinking was still an issue. So I finally stopped partaking in over-drinking and partying. This helped me to have a clear head to really be able to look at myself and my life.

I had attempted therapy earlier in my life but wasn't ready to really deal with my "stuff". But this time, I was ready. I started therapy again, with an amazing therapist who I will forever be thankful for. He helped me face so many things that I had pushed down my whole life. It wasn't pretty, and it was scary as hell. But I did it. I did the work. I fell into the darkest hole I'd ever been in and faced the most vicious monsters I had within me. But within that darkness, I found my light.

I had finally reached a point in my life where I was done. I was so sick and tired of feeling like a victim of my circumstances and the choices I was making that I was ready to face whatever demons laid waiting inside. I was ready to truly do the work and to live a better life.

Dealing with these things that I had tried to hide for so many years was difficult, to say the least. But I wasn't doing it alone. I had a lot of support in my life, thankfully. My husband, my family, and even though they aren't aware of all of it, my children. Looking back, I see now that my inner goddess was there with me the whole time. Supporting me, fighting for me and waiting for the moment that I would see her and embrace her. She never left my side.

While on my healing journey, I found a deep spiritual connection with the Universe, Spirit, and myself. Spirit, just like my inner goddess, was always with me, waiting for me to recognize the light within myself. But I was too far into the darkness to see it just yet. Perhaps I just wasn't ready to see it.

I always had an interest in spirituality, mysticism, magick and the healing arts but never thought to apply it to my life, or even how I would go about doing something like that. Thinking back, I remember many times that my Higher Self (my inner goddess) and Spirit nudged me towards these healing and supportive things. However, I was too much in my own head to recognize it at the time.

Through my journey of healing and spiritual connection, I realized that my purpose in life was to share my story and experiences with other women. To help uplift, inspire and encourage them on their own path. To hopefully be a supportive energy and guide in other women's lives.

Throughout all of my pain, healing and growth, I found my inner goddess. I found a confident, loving and powerful woman within myself. It's my hope to help you find your own inner goddess. Because all women, everywhere, deserve to feel like the complete, powerful and love-filled goddess that they are. Women everywhere deserve to live their best Goddess Life.

What is The Goddess Life?

The Goddess Life is living each day of your life doing something, no matter how small, to help you feel like the goddess that you are. Whether that be journaling, saying an affirmation, doing some yoga or dancing around your room in your underwear. Whatever it is, you do it in a way to help align your body, mind and spirit. You do things to help you tap into the goddess within you, so you can feel like the beautiful, powerful and loving divine woman that you are.

To me, a goddess is someone who:

- is empowered
- sure of herself
- embraces all aspects of herself (the light and the shadow)
- owns who she is
- embodies confidence
- expresses her creativity
- embraces her body and her sexual nature
- has a deep spiritual connection
- is supportive of others but knows when to place healthy boundaries
- operates from a place of love

Basically, she's a spiritually confident bad ass, in the most loving of ways.

We all have a goddess within us and we're all able to tap into the qualities of a goddess, whatever those qualities personally look like to each of us. Whether it's assertive, confident, loving, joyful, creative, sexual, nurturing or any other quality. Whatever qualities you feel embody a goddess, you have them within you. Our inner goddess is basically the most balanced and best version of ourselves. By doing small things each day, you can really nurture, heal, and align yourself so you can live the most empowered, happy and fulfilled life of your dreams.

To live The Goddess Life means to bring yourself closer to what you define as your own personal goddess. It means finding deeper spiritual connection and alignment.

***

Here's our first activity! Close your eyes and take a moment to center yourself. I don't want you to necessarily picture a goddess as much as I want you to feel a goddess.

What energy does this goddess embody? What qualities does she possess? How does she treat other people? How does she treat herself? Take note of what comes up for you. This will give you a good idea of how you envision your inner goddess. This is the goddess that lives within you.

If you'd like a guided meditation to connect with your inner goddess, head to www.cherisewilliams.com/thegoddesslife

***

Just as all women are different, so too are our inner goddesses. The qualities my inner goddess possesses may be different from yours and yours may be different than your friends. And that's okay!

That's what helps to make us all beautiful and unique.

Just as we all have our own special inner goddess, your inner goddess may change or evolve as you yourself change and evolve.

This book is aimed to help you tap into those goddess qualities within yourself so you can live your fullest and best life. Your body, mind and spirit in alignment. Not only does living your best goddess life benefit you, it helps to benefit the world. When we feel complete and confident, we walk around with our heads held high. We inspire other women to do the same. When we feel good about ourselves, we're able to more fully show up in the world. Because we've shown compassion to ourselves, we're able to more easily show compassion to others.

We're in a very interesting time right now. Our world is changing. More and more people are waking up to an aligned, holistic and spiritual way of life. Now, more than ever, the world needs more goddesses. The world needs more confident, assertive and loving women to help lead the way. And that's some powerful stuff.

So, not only can your own life drastically change for the better by connecting to and embodying your inner goddess, but the lives of your friends, family, and the world, can drastically change for the better as well.

Within this book you will find various inspiration and activities to help you embrace the goddess qualities within you, to help you to look at things from another angle, or to help you really connect with yourself. Some of the inspiration and activities may come a little easier for you than others, while some may be a little tougher. Some may bring up deep feelings or energies that you've had tucked away for years. It may not always be easy, but growth itself isn't always easy. But it's worth it. Oh, is it worth it.

So give yourself time and love with everything that comes up for you, the easier stuff and the not so easy stuff.

I suggest getting a beautiful journal or notebook, something special to use while reading and working with this book. In this journal or notebook you can write down anything that comes up for you during this process. Use this space to journal in, write down your insights from the activities and things that come up while reciting the affirmations. Or if you prefer, you can use the spaces within this book to record your journaling, thoughts and insights.

I've found that keeping a record of my spiritual work and growth can be quite powerful to look back on and refer to.

How to use this book:

I myself don't have the attention span to devote hours and hours every day to my spiritual growth, and I know I'm not alone here. More and more people in this day and age have short attention spans. That may not be the best thing, but it's the truth. So rather than beating ourselves up over our short attention spans, how about we try to work with them? I personally have found that even just five minutes each day can really help heal your soul, align yourself and really tap into the goddess qualities within. Whether it's by reciting an affirmation in the morning, reading a quote in the afternoon, journaling one page each day or doing a visualization exercise. I've found that it all adds up in a powerful and impactful way.

With this book, you can sit down and read it cover to cover if you so desire. However, I designed this book more with the intent of working with one page each day. Really soaking in the quotes, affirmations and doing the activities. Truly giving yourself those five minutes a day. Of course, if you want to devote more time to one of the activities or prompts, by all means, go for it! You're more than welcome to. But at the very least, spend a good five minutes of quality time with yourself, thoughts and feelings.

You can also use this book as a sort of oracle. Open the book and flip to a random page that you feel drawn to. Read and take in the wisdom or the lessons for that day and see how you can apply it to your life. But as with anything, it takes consistency. So, while you can grow your spiritual practice and align your mind, body and spirit with just five minutes a day, you really should be consistent with it. It's called a spiritual practice for a reason. We're practicing. And in order to get more proficient in whatever it is we're practicing, we must do it with consistency.

I've also found that by focusing my energy and thoughts on one piece of inspiration or one activity each day, I do it with a lot more intent. By giving myself 5-10 minutes each day to really devote to my inner soul work, my inner goddess work, I really give it my all during those minutes. Rather than trying to force myself to be in the spiritual moment for hours on end.

This isn't to say that a spiritual practice is always easy or quick. It's a lifelong process and journey. Our spiritual practice can be as deep as we allow it to be. Some days you may feel called to really dive within and spend hours in meditation or journaling. But this isn't required every day to have a powerful connection with Spirit and yourself. Some of my most profound "a ha" moments have been in a five-minute meditation or from reading a really good quote.

It's important as well that we integrate what we're learning and experiencing. We can sit down and read a spiritual self-help book from cover to cover or sit in meditation for hours on end, but unless we're actually giving ourselves a moment to sit with what we're learning, we won't really grow. Unless we give ourselves some time throughout our day to put into practice what it is we've learned, we won't really experience much or see many changes.

Within this book you will find affirmations, prayers, journal prompts, quotes and activities. We also talk a bit about chakras, crystals, tarot and oracle cards, and essential oils. These are tools and techniques that I used personally on my journey, and still use daily.

These various tools and modalities are in no way meant to "cure" you or to quickly fix your life. Rather, these tools and modalities are here to support you on your journey. You still have to do the work. You still have to walk your path, through the dark and the light. But hopefully the tools and modalities within this book can help support you on your journey.

And remember, if at any point in your life or journey you feel like you need even more support, please don't hesitate to reach out to a professional therapist or counselor. I always say, if you're even considering in the slightest that you should speak with a professional, you should go ahead and make that appointment. There's no shame in needing extra guidance.

It's my hope that there's a little bit of everything in this book for all of the many unique goddesses out there, no matter where you are on your spiritual journey.

You will get out of this book as much as you put into it. But remember, this is your personal journey and connection to your inner goddess. There is no right or wrong way to work with this book. Just go with the flow and do what feels right for you.

I am not a medical doctor. Nothing in this book is meant to treat, diagnose or cure anything. If you have any medical concerns, mental, emotional or physical, please speak to your healthcare professional.

A WORD ON CRYSTALS

Working with crystals isn't some new fad. People have been working with crystals for thousands of years. Use of crystals dates as far back as the ancient Sumerians, Egyptians and Greeks.

Modern science has tried to prove and disprove the healing power of crystals.

Science hasn't been able to explain everything, and there are plenty of new things that scientists are discovering each and every day. I mean, at one point, we had no idea about the concept of germs or microscopic organisms, until science proved it and discovered it. So who is to say that one day, science won't come up with a way to accurately measure the energetic properties and benefits of crystals?

Crystals are thought to promote balance within our physical, emotional and spiritual bodies. Because the energy formation of crystals is such a solid and stable energy frequency, outside influences don't affect them the way outside influences affect our personal energy fields. So the idea is, that by introducing the stable energy frequency of a crystal into our energetic space, it helps to balance and align our energy bodies.

Different crystals contain different types of energy. So, depending on what it is that you're working on, you would choose to work with a crystal that has a corresponding energy frequency. For example, if you're working on connecting to and trusting your intuition, you would benefit from choosing a piece of amethyst to work with. Amethyst vibrates at a similar frequency to the energy of intuition.

Even if you fall into the category of someone who doesn't believe at all in the power of crystals, they can still serve as a visual reminder.

As humans, we are visual beings. Keeping a piece of rose quartz near you for instance, may remind you every time you see it, to be a little more gentle and compassionate with yourself. Seeing a piece of fluorite on your desk may remind you to focus a little more on the work at hand. Because of these visual reminders, it helps us to stay the course and be accountable for our thoughts and actions.

Some people believe that crystals create a placebo effect, that is to say they don't actually work but the person using the crystal believes it does and so they actually see results. Our minds are a powerful thing. What we believe, we can achieve. So in my opinion, even if the crystal itself didn't energetically make a difference, it still technically worked. The person holding or using the crystal *believed* it would work, so it did.

Plus, crystals are pretty! Keeping pretty things in our homes and spaces can help raise our moods, which in turn raises our overall vibration.

Crystals can really do so many wonderful things for us on our spiritual journey. For example, crystals can help us connect to our spiritual team (angels, spirit guides, ancestors), align our chakras, connect to our higher-selves or help us work through our blocked feelings.

How should you use crystals in relation to this book?

In the back of the book, I have a list of various feelings, issues, chakras and emotions, and the crystals that correlate with them. You can refer to this list for anything in your life that comes up, or pair a crystal with the affirmations, prayers, prompts and activities in this book.

Will your meditations, activities and spiritual growth still be effective without the use of crystals? Of course! But if you can add another little layer to your practice, and you're feeling drawn to work with crystals, why not go for it? Worst case scenario, the crystal doesn't help your progress. Best case scenario, it adds a little more energy and support to your work.

Head to www.cherisewilliams.com/thegoddesslife *for a short video lesson on working with crystals*

A WORD ON CARDS

When you hear the word "tarot", you may picture a dark candlelit room, thick with incense smoke and a little old lady waiting to tell you your future. There are some tarot readers who embody this archetype, but reading cards is not always so mystical.

Tarot, oracle, angel and affirmation cards are all ways for us to tap into our subconscious and speak directly with our inner self, or our inner goddess. They're also a way for us to help translate messages from Spirit.

While cards can be used to see where certain energies are headed in your life or what energies you might expect in the coming days, nothing is set in stone. We have free will at all times and we are in control of what we do or don't do in our lives.

I personally view reading cards as a way to check in with yourself, the inner-you who we sometimes have a hard time hearing or listening to.

I got my first tarot deck when I was thirteen years old. Throughout my life, whenever I was feeling particularly stuck or lost, I would pull out my cards and do a reading for myself. I always found such comfort and guidance within the cards, not really realizing that I was tapping into my own intuition and inner goddess. As I got older and went deeper into my spiritual practice, I realized what a life-changing tool the cards are. They are a valuable asset to have on hand.

Whether you use tarot, oracle or affirmation cards is fine. It doesn't matter which type of cards you use, you can receive beautiful guidance and helpful tips from your Higher Self.

Cards are an excellent way to hear what your inner goddess has to say and to help yourself come up with a game plan of how you will move forward. Reading cards helps you tap into your intuition and begin to trust that gift. The more we use our intuition, the stronger it gets. Our intuition is always there to help us along in life.

Pulling cards for yourself can help you find some clarity or guidance on a situation. Sometimes, they serve as confirmation that you're on the right path. Whatever situation you're using the cards for, they can provide fabulous insight.

In the back of this book I've included various card spreads (questions) that you can use for different situations to help you find clarity and guidance. You can also pull some cards on any of the journal questions or prompts found within this book.

Remember, the cards and the messages they reveal are not the end all be all. It's up to you what you do or do not do with what the cards relay.

You can find a short video lesson on working with cards at www.cherisewilliams.com/thegoddesslife

A WORD ON CHAKRAS

Chakra is a Sanskrit word for "wheel". Our chakras are spinning energy wheels found within our bodies as well as our energy bodies (auras). We have many chakras, however people typically work with the seven main chakras.

These seven chakras make up our main chakra system. Starting at the base of our spine and ending at the top of our head, our main chakra system is aligned with our spine and center of our bodies.

The seven main chakras govern aspects of ourselves and our lives. When the energy is out of balance in any of the chakras, it can manifest as imbalance within our minds, bodies and spirits. This is why it's important to learn to work with these chakras. When we work with our chakras, they act as a guideline we can follow, to find where we may be having imbalances and how we can go about adjusting that balance.

For instance, if we're having a hard time communicating our feelings, we may have an imbalance in the throat chakra. This could even show up physically as a sore throat. Once we know that our throat chakra needs a little work, we can use specific tools and techniques to help us work through the energy there to find balance once again.

Our main chakra system covers everything from our basic needs and survival (the root chakra) all the way to our spiritual connection (the crown chakra), and everything in between.

I've personally found it very useful to do a daily chakra check-in. I take a moment to close my eyes and visualize each of my chakras. If one of them feels odd, appears to not be spinning well or isn't glowing brightly, I take note of it and see where in my life this imbalance may be manifesting itself.

I also like to tune in to my chakras when I'm having difficulties anywhere in my life. For example, if I'm feeling a little more anxious than normal, I know that my root chakra could use a little extra love and attention.

Our chakra system is a great guide for balancing our minds, bodies and spirits. And a balanced mind, body and spirit is the best way to embody that beautiful inner goddess of yours.

Within this book I've included some activities and inspiration relating to the chakra system. I've also included a list of the seven main chakras and a bit of information for working with each one, which can be found in the back of the book.

Want to learn a little more about the chakra system? Check out a short video lesson at www.cherisewilliams.com/thegoddesslife

A WORD ON ESSENTIAL OILS

Essential oils are one of the absolute best "tools" to keep in your Goddess Kit. Essential oils are a concentrated liquid that contain the plants chemical compounds. Sort of like the blood of a plant, quite literally the "essence". Along with the chemical compounds, this essence contains the aroma of the plant. Essential oils are considered nature's medicine.

Just as every plant is different, every essential oil is different as well. Each plant has its own chemical compounds which affect us differently.

The molecules within essential oils are so tiny, they can quickly and easily enter into our blood stream. Whether applying the oils to our skin or by smelling the oils from the bottle or a diffuser. This allows the chemical compounds in the oils to travel through our body and benefit various parts of our body system. This is great when using essential oils to balance our different body systems or for physical needs such as sleep or discomfort.

One of the most popular ways to use essential oils is for emotional benefits. Our sense of smell is directly connected to our limbic system in the brain. The limbic system is responsible for memories and emotions. So when someone smells cinnamon for example, it can instantly remind them of cooking pies with grandma in the kitchen as a child.

Our limbic system is also connected to parts of the brain that control our breathing, heart rate, blood pressure and more. This is why when we think of a stressful memory we can almost immediately feel our heart rate or breathing increase and our body tense up.

By using essential oils to trigger these parts of our brains, we can literally trigger our brains to feel more at ease, uplifted or more. And all of this happens within seconds. This is why essential oils can be so powerful and such an excellent tool to utilize in our self-healing.

Pairing essential oils with things like meditation or affirmations can be insanely effective. For example, if you're saying an affirmation to help you feel more calm, you could pair that affirmation with a calming oil such as lavender. This way, you're working with your brain verbally to feel more calm and also using an oil that stimulates your brain and body to be calm.

Not only are oils good for physical and emotional uses, they're wonderful for spiritual uses as well. Essential oils and aromatic herbs have been used around the world for centuries for many different types of religious and spiritual purposes. Essential oils help to raise our vibrations and connect us more deeply to Spirit and our inner goddesses. Reciting prayers or meditating and incorporating oils into that practice really adds something special. It helps to shift your mindset to one of deeper spiritual connection and can greatly benefit your practice.

Like crystals, essential oils aren't going to magically fix what you're going through emotionally. When using essential oils for physical purposes, like in the instance of ear aches, essential oils can definitely help remedy that. But our emotions are a little more tricky. While smelling an essential oil to help uplift your mood when you're feeling down can be helpful, you really do need to work on what it is that made you feel down in the first place. Essential oils are there to help support us on our journey, just like any other tool or technique we use.

I want to mention the importance of using high quality essential oils. There's a reason those essential oils you find at the grocery store are so inexpensive verses essential oils from a reputable company, that might be a little more pricey.

As of right now, there are no real legal guidelines that companies have to follow when marketing or labeling their essential oils. A company can legally label their oil as 100% pure, when in fact the bottle only contains a few drops of essential oil and the rest is filled with synthetic ingredients. Talk about scary! I don't know about you, but when I'm working with my mind, body and spirit, I don't want to rub a bunch of synthetic stuff onto my body or breathe it in through my nose.

There are many reputable essential oil companies out there. I highly suggest doing your research and choosing a company that resonates with you. I personally use dōTERRA essential oils, as well as Enfleurage essential oils.

Some essential oils are contraindicated for various health concerns. For example, if you're pregnant or nursing, there are some essential oils that should be avoided. Always check to make sure there are no contraindications before using essential oils.

A short video lesson on how to incorporate essential oils into your practice can be found at <u>www.cherisewilliams</u>*.com/thegoddesslife*

A WORD ON JOURNALS

Journals can be powerful transformational tools.

Rather than keeping in our thoughts and emotions, it's better to get them out. Writing in your journal gets these thoughts and feelings energetically out of yourself and your mind. In this way, you're able to release things that are no longer serving you. If we don't acknowledge things and don't get them out, they can eat us alive. Putting blinders on to our thoughts and emotions doesn't make them disappear. They're still there, bubbling beneath the surface. And until we deal with them, they will keep trying to make their presence known in our lives.

Get your thoughts and feelings out of your head and body and onto paper where you can visually see it. This can help you see your situations from a different perspective. I can't tell you how many times I've felt stuck in my mind or emotions, not knowing how to deal with them or even *why* I was having these thoughts or feelings in the first place. But once I started to journal about it, getting it out of my head, I was able to start to work through it. I was able to see things from a different angle. Journaling helps to make things click.

When writing in your journal, you don't have to use complete and proper sentences if you don't want to. Even just writing out adjectives of how you're feeling, or random words that relate to your thoughts, can be helpful. Some people find that scribbling or doodling helps them to process their thoughts and feelings.

The point isn't always about what you're writing or how you write it. The point is to get the energy moving. Get the energy from being locked in your mind and out of your head so you can start to process it and work with it.

Journals aren't just for when things are going wrong or you feel upset or depressed. Granted, this does seem to be a time when people journal the most, which is understandable. You're trying to get these feelings out and work through them. But it's important to journal as well when things are going *right* in your life. Because what we focus on is what we end up getting more of in our lives. If all we ever focus on is what's wrong, that's ultimately what we will get more of. This isn't to say that you shouldn't acknowledge your upsetting feelings. Like I mentioned above, we have to look at and face these feelings. But it's important to have a healthy balance of releasing and praising.

Journal five minutes each day, even if you feel you have nothing to talk about. Literally write about your day. Perhaps try to go a little deeper and think of one event from your day and how it made you feel. How did this event make others feel? The more we tap into our inner feelings and put words to them, as best we can, the more connected we then become to our feelings and also the feelings of others. And in turn, the more we get connected to our inner selves, the more we can begin to embody our inner goddess.

Within this book there are specific journal prompts for you to use. You may also find it helpful to read the quotes, affirmations and prayers and then journal about what comes up for you. After doing the activities in this book, it may be a good idea to journal about your experience with it.

Your journal is your own sacred space. Honor it, work with it and enjoy the connection it brings you with your inner goddess.

A short video lesson on how to incorporate journaling into your practice can be found at www.cherisewilliams.com/thegoddesslife

A WORD ON PRAYERS

Praying is a deeply personal experience, and there's no right or wrong way to pray. Simply do what feels right and feels natural for you and your connection to your higher-self and your higher power.

The prayers in this book vary to whom they are speaking to. I've used various terms to refer to our Source Energy. Whether it be God, Goddess, Divine Mother, Spirit, Universe, Angels or The Divine. Please feel free to exchange the term used for one that you are more comfortable with.

The prayers are closed out in various ways as well. Such as blessed be, and so it is, and amen. Again, please feel free to exchange these words for ones that are more comfortable for you or suited to your personal style.

You don't even need to be a religious person to pray or to benefit from prayer. Some people who have a hard time connecting to God or a source energy, or simply don't believe in it, find that praying is sort of a way to talk to your subconscious mind. Therefore, they still find benefit in praying. In a way, it's like telling your subconscious mind what you would like to have more or less of in your life.

They say praying to God is us speaking to God, but meditating is us listening to God. I personally find that after praying, it's a good practice to then take a moment to sit in quiet meditation. This can be for just a few moments, or longer. Listen to any messages or insights you receive. Take note of any feelings that arise. You may also find it helpful to keep a Prayer Journal. One where you can write down the prayer, or type of prayer, along with any insights or messages you received following the prayer. It's okay if you don't keep a journal. And it's okay if you don't immediately receive any sort of guidance or message. But I find that keeping this prayer journal is a great way to keep the flow of communication open between myself and The Divine.

Included with some of the prayers are crystal and essential oil recommendations. I enjoy pairing my words with crystals and oils. I feel it adds another layer of energy to the intention. Our words and thoughts are powerful indeed, and ultimately our thoughts are the only energy required. Please don't feel you must add any tools to your prayers to make them work. The oils and crystals I suggest are merely that, suggestions. If you feel called to use a different crystal or oil with the prayers (or none at all), please trust that and go with what feels good to you.

A short video lesson on how to incorporate prayers into your practice can be found at www.cherisewilliams.com/thegoddesslife

A WORD ON QUOTES

I absolutely adore quotes. Quotes are such an excellent way to receive quick but profound inspiration for the day. Quotes can sometimes help us put into words how we're feeling when we ourselves are lost for words, they provide some guidance for us. They can help us to see things in a different light, or to inspire us to think of things from a different angle.

Quotes can be as powerful as you make them.

I feel like quotes work best when you take some time with them. Rather than just reading a quote and then moving on with your day, take a moment. Read the quote. See what comes up for you and how it makes you feel. You can even take this time to close your eyes and do a short five-minute meditation on the words of the quote and just notice what comes up for you. Take out your journal and write down your thoughts and feelings. How does this quote relate to your life? If the quote doesn't directly relate to you, how could you incorporate the quote into your daily life?

Find a quote in this book that really resonates with you? Would love for you to share it on social media with others, using #TheGoddessLifeBook

A WORD ON AFFIRMATIONS

We're constantly talking to ourselves and the more we say something, the more we believe it. So when we're constantly telling ourselves "you suck" or "there's no way I would ever be able to accomplish that", the more we believe that nonsense. Likewise, the more we tell ourselves "I can achieve everything I put my mind to" or "I am a beautiful radiant goddess", the more we believe that truth. What we say to ourselves, becomes our affirmation.

Affirmations are more powerful when we say them with conviction and belief. It doesn't matter how awesome an affirmation is written, if it doesn't jive with us or it's worded in a way that doesn't feel authentic to us, then it's not really going to have much oomph. That being said, the affirmations within this book can be used as a template for you. If you don't resonate with how I've worded them, tweak the affirmation until it becomes something that totally resonates with your unique goddess vibe.

Affirmations work best when they're worded in a positive way rather than a negative way. For example, you wouldn't want to word your affirmation as "I will not doubt myself". All that is doing is confusing your mind. Your mind basically removes the word "not" and all it hears is "I will doubt myself". Instead, try wording it as "I always believe in myself". See how much more powerful and positive that sounds?

It's also good to note that affirmations tend to work best when worded in the present moment, not in the future. Use phrases like I am, I do or I can. This helps your mind believe that this is something you already are or something you already have, rather than something that may or may not happen in the future.

Short, sweet and to the point is good in regards to affirmations. Play around with the wording of your affirmations until you find what works for you. You may even find that you need to tweak the affirmation a bit as you're working with it. This is totally okay.

In order to really make the most of your affirmation and see the most positive change within your life, you can't really say the affirmation once or twice and then go about your day. Remember, we're always talking to ourselves, and we have a tendency to say not the nicest things to ourselves. A lot. In order to counteract possibly *years* of bad-mouthing ourselves, we need to put some work into these affirmations.

Saying the affirmation morning, noon and night is a good habit to get into. Try repeating the affirmation for at least three full minutes. You can do this while you're accomplishing other tasks as well. You don't necessarily have to sit there staring at a wall for three minutes while repeating the affirmation. For example, you can say the affirmation to yourself while preparing your morning coffee, driving to lunch or getting ready for bed.

Another good way to repeat the affirmation is in your journal. You can write the affirmation multiple times in your journal as you say it, out loud or in your mind. By writing the affirmation in your journal, this also gives you a chance to journal about anything that comes up with this affirmation. Perhaps noticing where in your body you're holding energy or any memories this affirmation may be bringing up.

If repeating your affirmation in first person isn't working for you, try switching it up! You could try speaking your affirmations in third person instead. For example, if I were saying my affirmation in this manner, rather than saying "I am a freaking powerful creator of my life!" I would say, "Cherise! You are a freaking powerful creator of your life!"

Sometimes, by hearing something said *to* us rather than *by* us, it makes it more believable and exciting. Even though technically, it *is* us saying the words.

A really powerful technique to incorporate with your affirmations is to use visualizations or to embody the feeling it evokes. When you're saying to yourself, "I welcome prosperity into my life with ease and joy", really tap into what it would feel like to have that prosperity flowing into your life. Visualize yourself with this increased abundance and the joy it brings you.

Another truly powerful affirmation technique is to try looking in the mirror, into your eyes, when saying your affirmation. This can be a little uncomfortable for some people at first or it may feel a little silly. It may even bring up some serious emotions for you. If it does, that's okay! It's important that we honor our emotions and respect that these things are coming up. It gives us a chance to acknowledge our feelings and to deal with them.

By looking yourself in the eyes while saying your affirmation, it's like speaking directly with your inner goddess. The eyes, after all, are the windows to our souls.

Something fun but very impactful you can do with your affirmation work is to try pairing your affirmations with corresponding crystals or essential oils. My personal favorite way to do this is by applying essential oil to my pulse points, while taking a few deep breaths of the scent and centering myself and my energy. I then hold the crystal while repeating my affirmation. This is helpful because the next time I smell that particular scent or see that particular crystal, it will remind me of my affirmation.

And finally, I've found the most success with affirmations by working with one topic at a time, rather than multiple affirmations for various topics. For instance, I may repeat three different affirmations but they will all be related to the same topic. Self-love, confidence or prosperity, for example. I find that this is less confusing for our minds and bodies.

Once whatever you're affirming has appeared in your life, or you begin to truly believe, accept and embody the affirmation, you can feel free to move on to a new one.

FINAL WORD

It's my hope that by bringing this book into your personal practice, you find a deeper connection to your inner goddess and find even more ways to embody her essence into your daily life.

Remember, you are beautiful and unique! You are a one of a kind goddess.

xxoo,
Cherise

INSPIRATION AND ACTIVITIES

Dearest Divine,

Thank you for giving me constant guidance and support. I appreciate the nudges and signs you give me. Thank you for steering me towards greatness and all that is good for me. I may not always know the exact destination of where I'm being guided, but I trust in you to always lead me on the correct path.

Blessed Be.

Affirmation

I AM CHOOSING NOW TO BE PROUD OF WHO I AM.

Crystal & Essential Oil Suggestion: Natural Citrine & Rosemary
Suggested Corresponding Chakra: Solar Plexus

Journal

What are three things in your life that you're thankful for?

1.

2.

3.

When life gets tough, keeping our eyes on what we're thankful for can really make all the difference. What we focus on is generally what we receive more of. The more we focus on what isn't going right in our lives, the more stress that will bring us, and ultimately the more things will seem to go wrong. By looking at what we're thankful for, it raises our energy and happiness, ultimately bringing more things into our lives to feel joyful about.

Refer back to this list whenever you're having a hard time seeing the good in your life. Feel free to add even more items to the list or switch things up every now and then.

"Don't put off your happiness for tomorrow. Create your happiness for the moment you're in today."

We aren't guaranteed tomorrow. We aren't even guaranteed the next hour or minute of our lives. So why would you put off your happiness for some time in the future? We can tell ourselves all sorts of things to postpone our happiness. Things like "well if I just get this one thing done, *then* I'll be happy" or "today is just too crappy of a day, I'll worry about happiness tomorrow".

Instead of thinking about the next thing or the next day, take a moment to be happy NOW. Happiness doesn't always have to be elaborate. What can you do for yourself right now, today, that can make you happy? Stepping outside and feeling the sun on your face? Going to the animal shelter and getting kisses from puppies?

The more moments of happiness, no matter how small, that we allow ourselves to experience, the happier we become as a whole.

Activity:

Make a list of some of the things you can do at any time to raise your happiness level. Refer to this list anytime you could use a boost of joy in your life.

Crystal & Essential Oil Suggestion: Angel Aura Quartz & Rose

"It's not always easy to look at ourselves and see when we're making excuses. You can take action and have success, or you can make excuses and remain stuck."

It seems it's always easier to blame outside circumstances than it is to own up to our own actions, or lack of actions.

This is just my luck! Nothing good ever happens to me. My life is just meant to be chaotic. Well if only somebody would've done something different, I wouldn't be in this situation. My childhood was shitty so now my life sucks.

These are things that people tell themselves when they aren't willing to take ownership of their own lives. Look, I get it! I used to be the same way. Blaming my crappy life choices and negative things in my life on everyone else. It wasn't until I decided that I wasn't going to be a victim to my life experiences anymore, that I started to find empowerment. It wasn't until I decided to stop using my past as an excuse to make poor life choices that I started to grow, heal, and find joy in my life.

Until you take ownership of how you react to your life, then you'll always be in victim mode. This isn't to say that some people aren't dealt some really crappy ass cards in life. Life isn't always roses, that's for sure. But it's what you do with your life that matters.

You can either choose to accept what life has handed you and let it keep you down, or you can take charge of your life and make the changes you desire. If you can't change the situation or the cards you've been dealt, you most certainly can change your thoughts and attitude about the situation.

How will you choose?

Journal Prompt:

Where in your life do you feel you may be making excuses?
What are you willing to do differently?

The wound is the place where the light enters you.

–Rumi

Dear God,

I could really use some guidance right now. Things aren't going quite how I expected them to go. And to be honest, it's a little frustrating and disheartening.

Please show me your guidance. Show me the way and your light.

Fill my heart with love and peace, for I know that all will be well with you by my side.

Amen.

"Dreams are your souls way of speaking directly to you."

Our dreams contain many messages and symbols. When we dream, it's a chance to hear directly from our souls. Keeping a dream journal is an excellent way to keep track of the guidance you may be receiving.

When keeping a dream journal, you don't have to necessarily write down your entire dream. If you find it easier, you can write down the things that immediately come to your mind. I personally find writing down the things that stick out in my mind is what works best. For example:

Bear, flowering tree, clear ocean water, moon, swimming.

I then take a moment to see if any of those words or activities have a personal meaning for me, or I will look up the symbolism of each.

This is such a fabulous way to receive guidance and support from The Divine and your Inner Goddess.

Activity:

Each morning, write down the symbols you remember from your dream the night prior. Keeping a journal right next to your bed is a good idea.

Do you notice any patterns in your dreams or symbolism? What do you think your soul is saying to you.

Affirmation

I AM CONFIDENT AND ASSERTIVE. I STAND UP FOR MYSELF AND OTHERS

Crystal & Essential Oil Suggestion: Black Tourmaline and Lemon
Suggested Corresponding Chakra: Solar Plexus

"The hardest step is the first. Once you make the choice to just go for it, the rest is just persistence. One foot in front of the other."

We don't always have to know our exact destination in order to begin on an amazing journey. Just knowing the general direction you want to go, can be enough of a plan to start with. Simply deciding that you want to make a change or you want to achieve something, and then going for it, is the biggest step.

Trust that you are divinely supported and will be guided along your journey. Especially if the journey seems to get difficult, because it will. But there are no great stories or adventures without some twists and turns.

Journal:

What is something that you've been wanting to do but have been putting off?

How would you feel if you actually took that first step?

How would you feel if you never began this journey?

Divine Spirit,

I know that if I can think myself into fear, I can think myself out of it. Help me to see the light in this situation and to switch my mindset from one of fear to one of love.

And so it is.

Affirmation

I AM A UNIQUE AND EXQUISITE HUMAN BEING. I EMBRACE MY UNIQUE QUALITIES WITH CONFIDENCE.

Crystal & Essential Oil Suggestion: Natural Citrine and Orange
Suggested Corresponding Chakra: Solar Plexus

Activity

AURA CLEARING

Our auras, or energy fields, are constantly absorbing and picking up energy. Even energy that isn't our own. From the spaces we enter, the emotions we have, the people we come into contact with, our auras can take on a lot of excess energy. Regularly clearing your aura is a good practice to get into. Here are two activities you can add to your practice.

1. Shower Clearing. This is one of my favorite ways to clear my aura. While taking a shower, imagine the water flowing down as a beautiful gold, silver or shimmery liquid. Envision this divine liquid pouring down you as it washes away any unwanted energy and leaves you shiny and cleansed. You may find it helpful to envision the unwanted energy flowing off you and down the drain.

2. Selenite Clearing. If you happen to have a selenite wand you can clear your aura at any time, pretty easily. Simply take the selenite wand, and holding it a few inches away from your body, scan your energy field with the wand. You may find it helpful to envision the energy from the crystal making your aura sparkle. As you're scanning your aura with the crystal, you're scrubbing away unwanted energy.

"Setting boundaries is a loving act"

Setting boundaries is an important thing in life, but one that a lot of us have a hard time with. Sometimes we tend to view setting boundaries as a selfish act. When in reality it's extremely unselfish. Setting boundaries comes from a place of love. When we set boundaries, we are showing ourselves love. We love and honor ourselves enough to say no when needed, in order to preserve our own energy or happiness.

Setting boundaries is also an act of love towards others. A lot of the time when we need to set boundaries, it's because the other person is taking too much from us or putting too much of their energy onto us. By saying no, and setting boundaries, it encourages the other person to be responsible for their own actions and energy. While that may seem somewhat harsh to some people, it really is a loving act. When people are responsible for themselves, it gives them a chance to grow and learn.

Affirmation:

I set loving and healthy boundaries.

Suggested Corresponding Chakra: Root & Solar Plexus

Activity

MINDFULNESS

What does it mean to be mindful? In its simplest term, it means to be aware. Be aware and notice the things going on around you and within you. When going on a walk, don't just fix your eyes straight ahead while thinking of what you need to get at the grocery store. Instead, be mindful. Notice how your feet feel on the ground as you take each step, feel the sun on your face and listen to the birds. Be present in the moment.

You can be mindful in any situation you're in. While doing the dishes, feel the water on your hands, notice how the soap bubbles up on the sponge.

Being mindful gives us a chance to be present in the moment and in our bodies.

Whenever you get the chance today, take a moment to be mindful of your body and your surroundings. Notice how it makes you feel.

"Each new day is a chance to begin again."

It's okay if today didn't go as planned. It's okay if you feel you didn't give it your all today. It's okay if today just flat-out sucked. Tomorrow is a new day. Each day we wake up is a chance for us to begin again. If you're not happy with how yesterday turned out, what can you do today to make it different?

Affirmation:

I greet each new day with a fresh mindset.

If we did all the things we are capable of, we would literally astound ourselves.

-Thomas A. Edison

Activity

POWER STAND

The way we hold our bodies and the way we stand, can really have an impact on our moods and energy levels. When we stand or sit hunched over, shoulders slumped, that's basically how our energy and mood feels. Slumpy and meek. But when we stand or sit with our shoulders back and spine straight, we feel strong and empowered.

One of the quickest ways to change your mood and energy level is to do the Power Stand, or Super Goddess Stand.

1. Stand with your feet flat on the ground and about hip width apart, feeling the soles of your feet connected to the earth.

3. Keep your back as straight as you can, with your shoulders back and head held high like the confident goddess you are.

4. Place your hands on your hips.

5. Stay in this position while you take five power breaths. Breathing in quickly and deeply through your nose (filling your abdomen with air) and exhaling deeply through your mouth.

6. Pair your breath and stance with an affirmation for an added boost.

Not only does standing in this position and posture make you feel confident, strong and empowered, but doing the power breaths helps to get the energy flowing and moving throughout your body.

It's helpful to do this exercise whenever you need a quick boost of confidence and power or whenever you're needing a quick energy shift.

When your solar plexus chakra is in need of some love and attention, that would be a great time to do the Power Stand.

Affirmation:

I am a confident and powerful goddess.

Suggested Corresponding Chakra: Solar Plexus & Root

"Sometimes we find ourselves at those crossroads in life. Where it seems everything has merged into one big intersection and we need to decide where to go next. Don't let these moments overwhelm you. Silence the mind, still the heart and go within. Trust that the pulls you feel from your higher self, from the Universe, and from Spirit will lead you in the right direction."

"Your story isn't over yet. It doesn't matter what chapter you're on, you can always write more pages."

Affirmation:

I am the creator of my life.

Spirit,

Help me to speak my truth with confidence and ease. Help me to share my heart and words with others. I know with your support, it is safe to speak up.

Thank you.

Crystal & Essential Oil Suggestion: Blue Kyanite & Peppermint
Suggested Corresponding Chakra: Throat

Activity

THROAT CHAKRA ACTIVATION

1. Take a moment to get comfortable and close your eyes.
2. Envision a bright blue light at the center of your throat.
3. Notice the light spinning in a clock-wise direction as the blue gets brighter and more vivid.
4. As the light energy spins and brightens, feel your throat chakra clearing.
5. Recite, out loud, the seed sound HAM (pronounced hum) or the vowel sound I (pronounced eye).
6. Keep reciting the sounds and visualizing the light until you feel your throat chakra has been sufficiently cleared and activated (at least three minutes, if not longer, would be a good idea).

Crystal and essential oil suggestion: Blue Calcite and Spearmint

Affirmation

I TRUST MY INTUITION. IT ALWAYS STEERS ME RIGHT.

Crystal & Essential Oil Suggestion: Sodalite & Juniper Berry

Suggested Corresponding Chakra: Third eye

"The things you say to yourself matter"

Pay attention to how you speak to yourself. The words and things you tell yourself become a mantra or affirmation. The more we hear something, the more we believe it. For instance, are you constantly telling yourself you're stupid?

I'm stupid, I should've known better.

This becomes your mantra or affirmation. Next time you catch yourself saying "I am…" and something negative follows, switch it up! Immediately tell yourself something positive instead.

I am smart and make the best choices possible.

While you may not believe it at first, the more your brain hears the positive affirmation, the more you will believe it and become it.

Activity:

What are some negative things you catch yourself saying to yourself?

Write down the most common negative things you say to yourself, then cross them out. Next to the negative affirmation, create a positive affirmation that you can use instead.

Universe,

I release the need for control in this situation. I know that everyone has freewill, including myself.

I know that I can't control the actions of others. I am responsible for my own actions.

I know that I can't control how others feel. I am responsible for how I feel.

I know that I can't control how others react. I am responsible for how I react.

I now release the need to control. For I know that I am safe and that you are supporting me.

Thank you.

"Sometimes we have to get lost in the dark in order to find our light."

Many of us wander around life without ever really knowing about, or harnessing the beautiful light within ourselves. But when we are plummeted into darkness, into hard times, it gives us a chance to discover that light.

We only have a few options when we're lost in the dark. We can continue to wander around while bumping into walls forever, we can succumb to the darkness (please don't ever let it get to that point, don't hesitate to reach out for help), or we can keep our eye on that light within.

Keep your eye on that light within, finding your way directly to it until you are holding it in your heart, bright as can be. Use that light to help guide yourself out of the darkness.

Even if it doesn't feel like it, you have a light within you. We *all* have a light within us. Sometimes we just have to get lost to find it.

<u>Affirmation:</u>

I hold onto my inner light and I let it shine.

Dear God,

I'm freaking amazing! Thank you for your support in helping me to achieve all that I have achieved in life! Thank you for gracing me with the gifts you bestowed upon me!

Love, me.

"The world is full of possibilities waiting for you to reach out and take them."

Sometimes we get so stuck on an idea or image of how we want something to be or look, that we close ourselves off to any other options.

Occasionally what is being provided for us is different than what we were anticipating. Trust that Spirit and the Universe are working for your highest good. Reach out and grab this new possibility. You may be surprised. It very well could be better than what you ever imagined.

On the flipside, sometimes we're so stuck in a victim mentality of nothing going right in our lives, that we are blind to anything good that may come our way.

When we're so focused on what is going wrong in our lives, we're missing out on all of the amazing things that the Universe is trying to give us. The Universe is constantly trying to provide us with possibilities. It's up to us to reach out and take them or to let them pass.

Affirmation:

I trust that the possibilities being given to me are of my highest good.

Affirmation

I SPEAK MY TRUTH WITH CONFIDENCE.

Crystal & Essential Oil Suggestion: Lapis Lazuli & Peppermint

Suggested Corresponding Chakras: Throat & Solar plexus

"The moment we silence our mind is the moment our heart speaks the loudest."

Our brains are constantly thinking. There's a lot of chatter that goes on up there. But when we take a moment to silence our mind, we can hear that our heart is speaking loudly.

Our hearts are pure love, whereas our brains can sometimes get muddled with negative self-talk and beliefs. It's important that we take time to hush the endless chatter and tune into that pure love within our hearts.

Our hearts will never steer us wrong. Our hearts are always communicating with us. All we have to do is give it a chance, and listen.

Activity:

Close your eyes for a moment and focus on your breath. Breathing in, breathing out. Calm and steady. Place your hand over your heart, feeling its energy. Breathe into this space. Notice what it feels like for you when you really tune in to your heart space. Listen for any cues or messages your heart has for you.

Suggested Corresponding Chakra: Heart

Dear Lord,

This earth, this world, this planet that we live on can feel scary as hell. But I know that even with all of the perceived darkness, fear and hate going on in the world, that ultimately we all come from a place of love.

I know that the more love I put out into the world, the more it will inspire others to put love out as well.

Each day I choose love instead of fear.

Amen.

Crystal & Essential Oil Suggestion: Malachite and Ylang Ylang

> "Sometimes things completely fall apart around us. It's in this time that we can build up stronger than before."

When things fall apart and it seems nothing is going right, that is the time to take a moment and see where you are. Things don't fall apart for no reason. Usually this is the Universe's way of stripping us of what is no longer serving us or what is no longer good for us.

While it can be painful or difficult, it really is a blessing in disguise. Use these times to really evaluate what it is that seems to be falling apart. Be honest with yourself on how this has served your life in the past.

Use whatever is falling away as a lesson to make you stronger and wiser for the future. Everything that happens to us can teach us something if we let it.

And remember, whenever something is removed from our lives, it creates space for something even better to come along.

Journal:

Is there anything currently in your life that is falling away? What lesson do you feel this is teaching you? What beautiful new energy will you bring in to this new space?

If nothing is currently falling away for you, think back to a time when you did feel this way. What lesson did you learn? Was anything new brought into your life in its place?

Dearest Spirit,

*Please work with me today so I may inspire others.
Please work through me today so I may encourage light
and love in all who cross my path.*

Blessed Be.

"You can feel sorry for yourself or you can do something about it. But you can't do both."

The cold hard truth: While you're busy throwing yourself a pity party, you could be using that energy to change the situation or change your mind-set about the situation.

I'm not saying that when something unpleasant happens that you don't let yourself feel all the feelings. Of course it's important to honor what you're feeling and let yourself process it. Everyone processes things differently and for different lengths of time.

But sometimes we let ourselves sit in the misery and sadness for longer than is needed. This is when it's really important to be completely honest with ourselves. Ask yourself: Am I truly still processing this sadness or unpleasant feeling, or am I just wallowing in my own self-pity?

Once you are done processing your feelings, wipe your tears and get to work. If the situation that made you upset is something that you have control over, then take that action! If the situation is something that you don't have control over, remember that you *can* control your mindset about it!

It's not always easy, but unless we want to sit around feeling sorry for ourselves all day, then it's what needs to be done.

Affirmation:

I am a strong warrior goddess who takes action in her life.

Affirmation

MY CREATIVITY IS BLOSSOMING AND I WELCOME IT INTO ALL AREAS OF MY LIFE.

Crystal & Essential Oil Suggestion: Carnelian & Orange

Suggested Corresponding Chakra: Sacral

Dear Spirit,

Please help me to release all that is not of my highest good. I'm tired of carrying this extra energetic baggage around. I have learned all that I can from this and I am ready to release it. Help me to release it so we can make room for new and beautiful things in my life.

Thank you kindly.

Don't grieve. Anything you lose comes round in another form. –Rumi

Activity

LOVING MORNINGS

A beautiful way to begin your day is to begin it with the energy of love. Before you even get out of bed in the morning, take a moment to tap into the energy of love.

You may wish to envision a pink light radiating around you while feeling a loving energy emanating from your heart center.

Trust that you are surrounded with love and that the Universe is supporting you.

By starting your day with this activity, you're putting yourself into a beautiful mindset before your feet even hit the floor.

You're opening yourself up to divine love, guidance and support. You're setting yourself up for miracles.

Affirmation:

I begin each day with the feeling of love and of being supported by the Universe.

Journal

What brings you the most joy?
What are you willing to do to feel that joy each day?

Crystal & Essential Oil Suggestion: Orange Calcite & Bergamot

Suggested Corresponding Chakra: Sacral & Heart

Activity

SING FOR YOUR THROAT CHAKRA

Singing is such a fabulous way to balance and activate our throat chakras. Today, take some time to sing your little heart out! Who cares if you don't have a Grammy award winning singing voice!

Singing not only activates and balances our throat chakras, it helps to raise our overall energy vibration. Higher vibrations equal more joy, which attracts more wonderful things into our lives.

Singing is also a great way to get energy moving. Singing vibrates our vocal chords which sends energy waves through our bodies. This helps to break up any stuck or stagnant energy within us.

Crystal & Essential Oil Suggestion: Aqua Aura quartz & Peppermint

Dear Lord,

I know that I can't do this on my own. I surrender the control, the pain and the fear to you. I welcome your guidance, love and support. Wrap me in your energetic light and help me to face all difficult situations that arise.

Amen and Blessed Be.

"Energy can get stuck in our bodies and become stagnant. It's important to physically move our bodies to get that energy flowing."

It really is amazing how much energy our bodies hold onto. Our memories, feelings and thoughts are literally stored within our bodies. So even when we're doing all of the mental and emotional work on ourselves, we can still sometimes feel stuck or find it's hard to really move on from whatever we're working on. This is because we need to release the energy from our bodies to truly release *all* of it.

Doing any sort of physical activity can help shake up and release that stagnant energy. I've found that various physical activities seem to stir up and release different types of emotions. For example, lifting weights or doing strength training seems to bring up the more deeply rooted old energies. Whereas doing something a bit "lighter", like dancing, seems to release fresher more surface energies. Play around with it and try different types of physical activities and see what comes up for you personally.

Affirmation:

I move my body each day to get the energy flowing.

"Your inner strength is strong as hell, even if you don't see it right now."

We are divine. We are made from the very fabric of the Universe. Inside each of us is a powerfully strong goddess. Even when it doesn't feel like we are very strong or we forget what we're truly capable of, our inner goddess remembers. Your inner goddess is there fueling your fire and ready to uplift you.

Whenever you find yourself doubting your strength, close your eyes for a moment and feel that fire in your belly. No matter how dim it may seem at first.

Connect to that fiery strong goddess within.

Affirmation:

I am a strong and confident goddess.

Suggested Corresponding Chakra: Solar Plexus

Our deeds determine us, as much as we determine our deeds

-George Eliot

"Forgiveness can set you free."

Forgiveness is a tricky topic. You always hear people talk about how forgiving someone doesn't mean that you agree with what they did, it's just a way for you to release them. But that's a hard concept to actually grasp sometimes, especially if what the person did was especially harsh or cruel.

But when we view each and every person as an extension of the Divine, as an extension of ourselves, it becomes a little easier to begin to forgive. And people are right, just because you forgive someone doesn't mean you agree with their act.

When we hold onto anger, fear, resentment and sadness it just leaves a hole within us. By forgiving, we release the hurt and replace it with love.

At our core, at our soul level, we are all love. Sometimes our human emotions and not the best choices get in the way of that love. But everyone deserves love and forgiveness.

Journal:

Is there anyone in your life that you could forgive? How do you think it would feel to finally release the hurt and replace it with love?

Suggested Corresponding Chakra: Heart

Activity

ROOT CHAKRA ACTIVATION

1. Get comfortable and close your eyes. Focus your attention to the base of your spine, your root chakra.
2. Imagine a deep red light, glowing brightly at the base of your spine.
3. Recite the sound LAM (pronounced "lum") or the vowel sound uh.
4. While you're reciting the sounds out loud, visualize the bright red light glowing brighter and brighter as it spins.
5. Continue this visualization and chanting until you feel the root chakra has been sufficiently activated, or for at least three minutes.

Crystal & Essential Oil Suggestion: Red jasper & Cedarwood

Dear Lord,

Help me today, and every day, to see the opportunities that I have before me. For there are many. I am thankful for all that I am able to achieve. I am thankful for the success in my life.

Amen.

"Honor your goals and don't give up when the road gets tough, but know when to ask for help."

When we set goals and intentions for ourselves, sometimes things go smoothly and seem almost effortless. But sometimes things don't always go as planned and the road gets difficult.

It's during the difficult times that we trust in the process and don't give up our dreams and goals. If it's something you truly desire to achieve or accomplish, you must press on.

It's important to be aware of when you need to ask for help. Sometimes on our journeys it's easy to feel like we're alone or that we have to accomplish it on our own. While yes, we ourselves must do the work, it's okay to ask for help every now and then.

Whether you're asking for spiritual help from your angels or spirit guides, or you're asking for help from another human being, support is a beautiful thing.

Affirmation:

I honor my goals and ask for help when needed.

"Follow your happiness. When you follow your happiness, the Universe clears paths for you to greatness."

It sounds simple and maybe even a little cliché. Follow your bliss, follow what lights you up, follow your happiness. But man, is it powerful when you do follow your joy.

Our happiness is sort of like a built in radar system for us. It leads us to things that are for our highest good. By following what makes you happy, you can achieve amazing things! Things that perhaps you hadn't even thought of or planned on.

Not only that, but when we follow what makes us happy, it raises our overall energy vibration. When our energy vibrations are raised, we become more of a match for the awesome things in life that we desire. It's almost like the universe clears paths for you to have and experience beautiful things when you follow your joy.

Journal:

What makes you happy? Do you follow your joy or do you tend to question it?

Affirmation:

I follow my joy and trust that the Universe will provide.

When I admire the wonders of a sunset or the beauty of the moon, my soul expands in the worship of the creator.

-Mahatma Gandhi

"If you think you don't have enough, then not enough is what you'll always have. If you focus on the abundance in your life, then abundance is what you'll have."

Whatever we focus on in our lives is what we tend to have more of. When we look at our lives, if all we ever see is what we "don't" have, then we will never be happy and we will always feel like we are lacking.

But if you look at your life and notice all of the abundance around you, then you will feel happier and more secure, which in turn creates more abundance.

When we're in the habit of noticing lack, we're basically training our minds to notice even more lack, which makes us feel miserable.

But when we're in the habit of noticing abundance, we're training our mind to notice even more abundance around us. This makes us feel joyful and thankful.

A joyful and thankful person naturally attracts more things into their lives that make them feel joyful and thankful. Consequently, a miserable person who feels they're lacking in life will naturally attract more things to make you feel even more miserable.

It isn't always easy at first to notice the abundance around us. Especially if your bank account is low and bills are due. Trust me, I've been there. But when we really start looking at all of the good in our lives, we realize that we really are pretty well off and have abundance in our lives.

The fact that you're reading this book can be seen as abundance and something to be thankful for. The fact that you can *read* is awesome. The clean water you have access to, electricity, shoes on your feet, happiness, health…abundance is all around us, big and small.

Activity:

Make a list of all of the abundant things you have in your life that make you feel thankful and joyful.

Suggested Corresponding Chakra: Root

Beloved Spirit,

May my intuition be strong.
May my heart radiate love.
May I trust in the divine guidance I receive from you.
May I always speak with honesty.
May I be confident and keep my head held high.
May I be nurturing and kind.
May I keep my head in the clouds with my feet firmly on the ground.

Blessed be.

KINDNESS MATTERS

We all have chances during the day to help make someone else's day a little brighter and to be a little more kind to another human being or living creature. We never know what someone else might be going through, and it really doesn't take much to add a little more love and kindness to someone else's day.

By brightening another's day, not only does it make them feel better, it makes us feel better as well. It's a win-win situation. And let's be honest, the world could always use a little more kindness.

Activity:

Make a list of 5 things you can do today to make someone else's day a little brighter.

1.

2.

3.

4.

5.

"Nothing brings clarity to our entire being quite as much as immersing ourselves into nature."

When we get out into nature, it sparks something within us. It reminds us of our primal nature, it reminds us that we are connected to something far bigger than ourselves, and it helps us feel grounded and secure.

When we go out into nature we are able to truly align our minds, bodies and spirits.

Between the alignment, the grounding energy and the extra oxygen the trees, plants and fresh air provide us, it's no wonder that people feel so refreshed after spending time outside.

I know for me personally, any time that I'm feeling stuck in my life or like I'm walking around in a fog or a slump, I head out into nature. Each and every time, I emerge feeling clear-headed and secure.

Activity:

Whether it be the woods or a beach, head out into nature. Take note of how you're feeling prior to going out and how you feel after spending some time outdoors with Mama Earth.

Crystal & Essential Oil Suggestion: Tree agate & cypress

Activity

DANCING FOR THE SACRAL CHAKRA

One of the best ways to get stagnant sacral chakra energy moving, is by moving your body. Particularly dancing in a seductive fashion with lots of hip rolls and booty pops.

Today, and whenever your sacral chakra could use some fresh energy, turn on some music that makes you feel beautiful and sensual.

Move your body, focusing on anything that moves your hips, buttocks and sacral region.

Don't worry if you feel silly at first, this dance is just for you. Close your eyes if it helps you get more into the moment.

See where the dancing and the movement leads you. See what energy or thoughts come up for you while you continue to move the energy in your body.

Continue dancing and moving your body until you feel the energy is flowing.

You may find it helpful to journal your thoughts and feelings following this activity.

We are what we repeatedly do.
Excellence, then, is not an act, but a
habit.

–Aristotle

Thank you Divine Spirit,

Thank you for making me, me.
Thank you for my personality, my body, my life, my lessons, my experiences.
Thank you for making me truly unique.
Thank you for giving me gifts that only I possess.
Thank you for allowing me to share those gifts with others.

Thank you.

"The power to save yourself is within you."

We can utilize outside help when we're working on ourselves, but ultimately it's an inside job.

We can use all of the crystals and oils we want, we can read all of the books we think we need and we can see all of the counselors under the sun, but until we're ready to put the work and effort in, we won't see any real changes within ourselves or our lives.

For a couple of years in my early twenties I was seeing a therapist. I'm thankful I was seeing her because who knows how much worse off I would've been without her support. However, I saw zero improvement in my life or the poor choices I was making. I saw no improvement in my self-sabotaging ways and deep sadness. I wasn't getting any worse, but I wasn't getting any better.

About ten years later I started seeing a new therapist. This time around I did see improvement in my sadness, life choices and overall quality of life.

Why was this time different? Because I was finally ready to do something about how I was feeling. I was ready to step up and tap into my inner power. Even when it felt like I had no strength to face what needed to be faced, I faced it. Which in itself helped me feel stronger.

The point is, that while therapists, meditation, crystals, oils and other modalities can most certainly help aid the process and offer you support, it's ultimately up to *you* to tap into your inner power and make the changes you wish to see.

You can't continually search outside of yourself for your strength or validation. To really make the big changes in life, you've got to tap into your own power. And trust me, you've got so much strength and power inside of you. Sometimes it just takes a little longer to recognize it.

If you're thinking at all that you should seek professional counseling, please do. Even if you're not quite ready to step into your personal power and make life changes. I really have no idea how much worse I would've gotten had I not been seeing a professional.

Suggested Corresponding Chakra: Root & Solar Plexus

"Stop silencing yourself and your ideas in order to please and appeal to others. The world needs your unique voice and thoughts."

We are all different. What makes us different is what makes us unique and special. And the world needs special.

The thing is, it doesn't matter what we say or don't say, there will always be some people who disagree with us. Just as there will always be some people who agree with us.

We can't please everyone. So the best thing to do is to share your unique thoughts with the world. You never know who is listening. You never know who needs to hear your words.

Affirmation:

I speak my ideas with confidence and grace.

Suggested Corresponding Chakra: Throat & Solar Plexus

My dearest Spirit,

Thank you for another day of life. Thank you for all of the blessings and lessons today has taught me. I'm looking forward to what tomorrow holds. I'm thankful to have you by my side. Thank you for your guidance, love and support.

Blessed be.

"We can't escape our feelings. It's best to just face them head on than to dance around them."

Even when we try to bury and ignore them, our feelings are still there. And until we face our emotions and deal with them, they will continue to pop up in our lives, demanding to be dealt with. Eventually everything comes to light.

Once we face our feelings, thoughts and emotions, we can begin to move on from them. We can begin to integrate their lessons into our lives, and they no longer hold power over us.

Journal:

Is there anything in your life that you've been burying inside of yourself?

What will it take for you to face those feelings?

"Rather than doubting your creativity, just go with it and see where it takes you."

We all get creative nudges from time to time. But a lot of us start to question the creative idea or even doubt that we would be able to execute it.

Creativity doesn't care about your skill level. Creativity doesn't care how "good" or "bad" you think you are. Creativity just wants you to create.

Next time you get a creative idea, just go with it, and see where it takes you. Creativity is just another form of energy, and in order to get that energy moving and flowing, we have to allow ourselves to tap into it and express it.

When energy is flowing it can lead to new ideas or even help us to work through old energies that have been stuffed down and ignored.

We don't even need an end purpose to create. Create just for the experience of creating.

Got an idea to paint a picture? Pull out those paints and get to painting! Got an idea for a poem to write? Take out a pen and paper and get to writing!

Suggested Corresponding Chakra: Sacral

Dearest Universe,

I am letting go of the outcome. I have put forth my wishes, dreams and desires. It's in your control now and I know that you will send only the best outcome into my life.

Amen!

Activity

MIRROR WORK

This is a popular activity that is simple but powerful. This activity is wonderful at helping you to really get in touch with your Inner Goddess. It also helps connect you to your heart chakra to facilitate self-love, compassion and confidence.

1. Take a moment when you won't be disturbed. Turn off the phone and television.
2. Hold a mirror about a foot in front of your face so you can clearly see your eyes.
3. Look into your eyes and hold your gaze for at least two full minutes.
4. Make sure to actually look deep within your eyes, to your soul.
5. Take a moment to see what comes up for you. Try not to judge the thoughts and feelings that come up. Simply witness them.
6. Before you put the mirror away, say a few nice things to yourself. For example: I am worthy. I am beautiful. I love myself.

Try this activity every day for a month and you'll notice a deeper connection and love for yourself.

Crystal & Essential Oil Suggestion: Rose quartz & Thyme

Dear God,

*Sometimes my family and loved ones get on my nerves.
But I know that they're most likely coming from a place
of love. Please help me to release their opinions of me
and release their baggage from my life. Help me to send
them love.*

Amen.

"We are spiritual beings. But we are also human beings."

Somewhere along the line in certain areas of the spiritual community, our humanness became something to be frowned upon. Love, light and ascension were something to be honored and the shadow, raw emotion and human feelings became something to shun.

This is not a healthy way to live.

We are most certainly spiritual beings, striving towards a deeper spiritual connection, but we are also humans. With human bodies and human emotions. It's a bit ridiculous in my opinion to try and ignore our very human essence.

Should we try to be the best versions of ourselves that we can be? Of course. Should we continue to deepen our spiritual connection and soul growth? Definitely.

But we can't ignore our very real human emotions and needs. We have these feelings and needs for a reason. There's no reason to beat ourselves up for having them. It's what we do with our feelings that matters.

Work through your feelings, feel them, honor them. The light *and* the shadows.

Affirmation:

I honor and embrace my human nature

Journal

What bad habits do you feel you have?
How are these habits holding you back in life?
What would it look and feel like to conquer those bad habits?
What are you willing to do to commit to removing these bad habits?

"If you wait until you're not afraid to do something, you may be waiting forever. Use the fear as excitement and energy to propel you forward."

I don't know a person around who hasn't had some sort of fear or hesitation before they attempt something new. It's a normal human reaction. But it's the people who don't let this fear and hesitation hold them back that end up doing some pretty awesome things.

Fear and anxiousness are just a form of energy. Instead of using that energy to continue to hold you back, switch that energy to one of excitement. Try using that new exciting energy to help you achieve whatever it is that you're aiming for.

Journal:

If you knew it was 100% possible to achieve, what would you want to do in your life? Why do you think you're holding back? How could you use that hesitation as a strength?

Beloved Divine,

I am ready and willing to bring love into my life and into my heart! I welcome this love into my life in whatever way you see fit.

With love, me.

Activity

SOLAR PLEXUS ACTIVATION

1. Get comfortable and relaxed in a quiet room where you won't be disturbed. Close your eyes and take a few deep breaths.
2. Envision a beautiful yellow light glowing about two inches above your belly button.
3. See this bright yellow light spinning and becoming more and more vivid. Feel the energy being cleared and moved within this chakra.
4. Recite out loud the seed sound "ram" pronounced as "rum". You could also repeat the vowel sound ohh.
5. Keep reciting and visualizing until you feel this chakra has been sufficiently cleared and activated.

Crystal & Essential Oil Suggestion: Pyrite & Grapefruit

"Self-care is more than bubble baths and pedicures."

Bubble baths, pedicures, taking yourself to the movies or treating yourself to a relaxing night in are all excellent ways to take care of yourself. And those types of activities are needed. But there's more to self-care than that.

Self-care also means you set healthy boundaries for yourself. Self-care is saying no to things that you don't want to do. Self-care is honoring and working through your feelings. The pleasant ones, and the not so pleasant.

So, while it's good to pamper yourself every now and then or do things that you enjoy, don't forget to take your self-care game to a deeper level.

Journal:

What are some of the ways that you take care of yourself? What are some things you could do to take it to an even deeper level?

Journal

Are there any truths about the world, or yourself, that are hard to acknowledge? Are these ultimate truths or are you able to shift your mind about them?

Dearest Spirit,

Allow me to receive support. Support from others and support from you. I know that asking for support is not a sign of weakness, but a sign of strength.

Amen.

"Mindset matters."

Mindset is pretty damn important. If we aren't in the right mindset when working towards a goal, we will have a very difficult time achieving that goal. We may give up much quicker when things get tough. But with the right mindset, we can achieve great things. With the right mindset, even when things become difficult, we keep on going.

I've noticed that pretty much every time I start to get frustrated with something I'm working on or something I'm manifesting, that it's my mindset getting in the way.

I take a moment to regroup and switch my mindset. Going from a place of frustration or feeling like I can't do something, to a place of knowing that I can and will accomplish what I set out to do.

Sometimes it takes a big pep talk to myself or reciting some affirmations, but it never fails. Each and every time I switch my mindset, miracles happen.

Next time you find yourself frustrated or stuck, take a moment to check out your mindset. Then set about to change it.

Affirmation:

I can achieve whatever I set my mind to.

Activity

BODY LOVE

This can sometimes be a tough subject for women. Our bodies always seem to be evolving and changing, and whether it be from societal pressures or old wounds from our younger years, we tend to have a lot of disdain for our bodies.

A good way to begin loving our bodies, or even deepening the love we already have, is to touch our bodies. Not necessarily in a sexual way either, but in a sensual and intimate way.

Get to learn your body. The curves, the lumps, the scars, the smoothness. All of it. The more in touch (literally) that we get with our bodies, the more we can begin to form that emotional bond with them.

I've talked to some women who say they rarely, if ever, touch their bodies in a comforting or sensual way. I used to be the same way until I participated in Mastering Message Embodiment, a program with Ciara Rubin. In this program she urged us to get to know our bodies in a sensual way. This action helped me form an even deeper bond with myself and begin to honor *all* of me.

For this activity you'll want to have some alone time where you won't be disturbed. Maybe turn the lights down low and light candles, whatever makes you feel comfortable.
The first few times you do this exercise you can do it fully clothed, or not. It's your decision. But ultimately you want to eventually do this exercise in the nude, to really get to feel your body.

Begin to touch your body in a comforting or sensual manner. Running your hands down your arms and legs, massaging your lower back or abdomen, cupping your breasts, lightly stroking your fingers along your body. Whatever feels good or natural.

You may find that doing this exercise with your eyes closed may help you really feel in to what your body is saying to you. Alternatively, you may find that keeping your eyes open and really looking at your body is powerful. Try it both ways and see how you feel.

This may be a very deeply moving experience for you. Honor it and whatever comes up for you. Try not to be judgmental of your body. If those thoughts come up, simply be aware of them and then push them to the side. You can always journal about those feelings afterwards.

Before you end your body love session, as you continue to massage or stroke your body, tell your body loving words. You don't necessarily have to believe these words right now. But the more you get in touch with your body and pair it with kind words, the deeper your connection and love will become for yourself.

Affirmation:

I appreciate and honor my body.

"The truth isn't always easy, but it's the right thing to express."

The truth isn't always easy to say. When we don't speak the truth, it's usually because we're afraid of hurting the other person's feelings or we're trying to protect ourselves in some way.

But when we don't speak the truth, we're really hurting every party involved. By not speaking the truth to another person, we're not giving them a chance to learn or grow from the experience. Sure, sometimes someone might get upset at the truth you speak to them, but it's not up to you to control how another person feels or reacts. As long as the truth you're speaking is genuine and from a place of love, I believe it's the right thing to express.

And when we bite our tongues and don't speak the truth to another person, it ultimately hurts us. It invalidates our own feelings and almost forces us to shrink down our energy. It's not a good feeling.

Next time you have the chance to speak a truth, instead of silencing yourself, try going the truthful route instead.

Journal:

Do you feel there is ever a time that telling a lie is okay? Why or why not? Would you prefer people always told you the truth?

Affirmation:

I speak the truth with confidence and love.

Corresponding Chakra Suggestion: Heart Chakra and Throat Chakra

Divine Mother,

Please help me to open my heart. Please help me to offer love. For I know the more love I give, the more love I receive. Please help me to embody empathy. Empathy for others and empathy for myself.

Love, Me.

Activity

HEART CHAKRA ACTIVATION

1. Get comfortable in a seated or reclined position. Make sure that all distractions are removed and electronics turned off.
2. Envision a beautiful green light radiating at the center of your chest. See this green light spinning, and as it spins the color glows brighter and brighter.
3. Recite, out loud, the seed sound yam (pronounced "yum") or the vowel sound ah (as in the word "saw").
4. While you repeat the sounds, continue to visualize the bright green light as it spins. Feel this chakra clearing of any stagnant energy.
5. Recite and visualize until you feel this chakra has been fully cleared and activated, or for at least three minutes.

Crystal & Essential Oil Suggestion: Rhodonite & mandarin

"You don't want to look back on your life and think of all the things you could've done but didn't."

Time is fleeting. I don't think I have to really tell you that. Our time on this earth, in this body, is extremely short in the whole grand scheme of things. I can only imagine what it would be like to be at the end of my life, looking back and regretting not taking chances on things. To feel like I didn't truly take advantage of the opportunities and life given to me.

When we look at it that way, it sort of helps remove fear from any situation we might be faced with. Sure, we will still have some fears and hesitations about experiencing new things. But if we keep it in our minds that we aren't promised tomorrow, we may be a little more likely to actually get out there and live life to the fullest, whatever that looks like for you.

Journal:

Do you feel as if you have truly lived? What would make you feel more alive?

Is there anything from your past that you're glad you did when you had the chance? Alternatively, is there anything from your past that you had the chance to do, but didn't? What did both of those experiences teach you?

Dearest Goddess,

Help me to see the good in this situation. Help me to see the silver lining. Even though this situation isn't quite what I expected, I know that some good can come from it. Help me to see the lesson and apply it to my life.

Many blessings

Thousands of candles can be lit from a single candle, and the life of the candle will not be shortened. Happiness never decreases by being shared.

–Buddha

"It's not your responsibility to make people like you."

It doesn't matter who you are or what you do, there will always be people who just don't resonate with you. And that's okay! Do you truly like everyone you meet? Probably not. It's not up to you to make sure everyone likes you.

If you try to make everyone like you, you'll end up with a lot of people who probably don't like you. Or at the very least, don't feel really connected to you. Because they won't know *you* or what you stand for or what you're really into.

But if you stop worrying about pleasing everyone, and instead work on liking yourself, the right people will want to be around you. You will exude confidence, happiness and authenticity. And people really dig that. The *right* people will want to be around you, for *you*. The real you. Goofy personality, quirks and all.

Affirmation:

I release any need to please others. The only person I need to please is myself.

Crystal & Essential Oil Suggestion: Sodalite & Siberian Fir

"It takes a lot of strength to be vulnerable."

Some of the strongest people I know are the ones who aren't afraid to show their vulnerable side. Being vulnerable isn't a sign of weakness, it's a sign of courage.

Courage to stand up and let others know that you are a human with feelings. You're a human with heart and soul. Not everyone has it all together. Sometimes people crumble, sometimes people get scared and sometimes they get upset.

There's no sense in trying to hide those feelings, especially when we all experience them.

Being vulnerable can feel like a scary thing sometimes. But softening and opening up to those vulnerable feelings rather than keeping yourself hardened, can create room for some beautiful growth to occur.

Journal:

Do you feel like you express your vulnerability? Why or why not? How do you feel about others who show their vulnerable side?

Suggested Corresponding Chakras: Heart and Solar Plexus

"We've only got one body in this lifetime. Try your best to honor it."

While we are in this life, we are blessed with only one body. But so many of us spend a lot of time hurting and hating this body, regardless of its physical condition.

We can love and honor our bodies at all of its phases. This is a concept that was a hard one for me to grasp for a long time. I felt that once my body looked a certain way, *then* I would love and honor it. But I soon realized that with that mentality, my body would never be good enough. No matter how fit I got or how much weight I lost.

I realized that to truly love and honor my body, I had to love and honor it at all of its phases. I learned that by loving and honoring my body, I wanted to do good things for it because I loved it. Not because I hated it. And this mentality feels so much healthier and happier.

Affirmations:

I love my body and all that it does for me.

I honor my body and all it has been through.

I treat my body with respect.

Spirit,

I release judgment. Judgment of others and judgment of myself. I know everyone is going through life with their own set of trials and tribulations. Who am I to judge another. I release this judgment and ask you to help me replace it with love.

And so it is.

Activity

MOONLIGHT BATH FOR THE THIRD EYE

Our third eye (where our pineal gland is located), loves the moon and its energy. By bathing our third eye in moonlight, we can help awaken and strengthen our pineal gland and third eye chakra.

On a clear night, especially potent during a full moon, go outside or stand in front of a window.

Let the moonlight stream down onto your face.

Take a moment to watch the moon. Study her shape, the light, and her appearance. Notice how her light dances across the clouds or trees.

Close your eyes and feel the moonlight radiating into your third eye chakra. You may even notice your forehead begin to tingle or get warm.

Feel and envision your third eye absorbing this potent moon energy.

Continue to bath in the moonlight until you feel your third eye has been sufficiently charged.

Crystal & Essential Oil Suggestion: Moonstone & Lavender

"You don't need to listen to everyone's opinions. The only opinion that matters is your own."

So many people seem to be full of suggestions, thoughts and opinions surrounding our lives. But ultimately, their opinion doesn't mean squat.

Your life is your life. You are the only one who will be living it. So, your opinion is the only one that really matters.

Of course, sometimes we turn to others for advice. And sometimes, that advice is given whether we ask for it or not. But take it all with a grain of salt.

Whatever decisions or choices you make in regards to your life, are your responsibility alone.

Affirmation:

I make healthy choices for my life.

Affirmation
I AM A SENSUAL AND SPIRITUAL GODDESS.

We are allowed to be divinely spiritual and at the same time, deeply sensual. In fact, for a lot of traditions in the world, these two aspects are deeply related.

It sometimes seems in our western world, that sensuality and sexuality have been made out to be something that is shameful. Especially if you're a woman. Therefore, a lot of women feel as if they can't possibly be spiritual and embrace their sensuality at the same time.

But this couldn't be farther from the truth.

Our bodies were made to feel pleasure. Feeling pleasure releases all kinds of happy hormones in our bodies and brains. It helps to raise our energetic vibrations. And in turn, can actually help to connect us even more deeply to various spiritual vibrations.

So, embrace the sensual goddess that you are. There is no shame in enjoying this body that you have been gifted.

Crystal & Essential Oil Suggestion: Unakite & Jasmine

Dear God,

Please help me to empathize with the struggles of others. Please help me to put myself in their shoes and see the situation from their point of view. Please help me to open my heart with compassion. To give love where there is judgment. To give peace where there is chaos.

Amen.

"In order to truly appreciate the light, we must know what it's like to face the darkness."

Activity

CROWN CHAKRA ACTIVATION

1. Get in a comfortable position in a quiet space where you won't be disturbed.
2. Close your eyes and envision a beautiful white light at the crown of your head. See this white light glowing brighter as it spins.
3. Feel this white light clearing your crown chakra of any stagnant energy.
4. While envisioning the light spinning, say out loud the seed sound om (pronounced aum) or the vowel sound eee.
5. Continue envisioning the light while chanting the sound for at least three minutes, or until you feel your crown chakra has been sufficiently activated.

Crystal & Essential Oil Suggestion: Clear Quartz and Frankincense

"Some of the most beautiful transformations happen in the shadows."

The light isn't better than the dark, and the dark isn't better than the light. In order for either to exist, the other must be present.

In the spiritual and holistic communities, sometimes a lot of emphasis is put on the light. Honoring the light and living in the light. And while being in the light is a great place to be sometimes, we must also honor the darkness and not be afraid to dive into the depths.

By being comfortable going into the darkness, we are then able to have the most beautiful transformations. Majority of transformations happen from our journey's into the dark.

We can then take what we learned in the darkness, and apply it to life in the light. A perfect balance.

Affirmation:

I honor the dark and the light within me.

Journal:

Where in your life has a visit into the dark led to something beautiful?

"The more connected you become to your spirituality, the more connected you become to yourself. You find yourself."

A lot of people, myself included, begin on a spiritual path in order to feel connected to something outside of themselves. To find connection, support and meaning within our Universe and life.

But something beautiful happens when we open ourselves spiritually and begin to find connection and support: We find connection and support within ourselves.

We discover a deep love and strength within ourselves, and we learn that spirituality isn't just something "out there" to be discovered. Spirituality is within us.

Suggested Corresponding Chakra: Crown

Dear Spirit,

Help me to embrace my quirks and my differences. I know that my quirks and my differences are what make me unique. I know that when I embrace my quirks and differences, I will be stronger and happier.

Many thanks.

Activity

HUG A TREE

This may feel a little goofy to some, but this is a really great and easy activity to do to ground your energy.

Head outside and hug the first tree that you feel drawn to. If hugging the tree really isn't your thing, then simply placing your hands on the tree will work as well.

Hug the tree, or place your hands on it, and simply breathe. Take in some deep breaths, with your eyes open or closed, and feel the strength of the tree.

You may even wish to envision the roots of the tree, growing deep and strong into the earth. Feel this rooted energy entering into your energy space.

When doing this activity, I like to give the tree some love as a thank you for helping to root my energy. I'll simply think loving thoughts to the tree or visualize a beautiful pink light surrounding it.

You can do this activity any time you're feeling a little unstable, anxious or uprooted.

Suggested Corresponding Chakra: Root

"Putting yourself first is an act of love."

It's okay to put your needs, wants or desires first at times. We can't possibly expect to be at our best if we are in the habit of always putting ourselves last.

If we always put others first, we will eventually feel depleted and down. And if we're feeling depleted or down, we won't be operating at our best. How on earth can we possibly be a help to anyone else, or ourselves, if we're feeling rundown and neglected?

Putting yourself first is an act of pure self-love. And we all deserve a little love.

Journal:

Do you struggle with putting yourself first and showing yourself the compassion you deserve? Why do you think that is or isn't so?

Suggested Corresponding Chakra: Heart chakra

Crystal & Essential Oil Suggestion: Botswana agate and juniper berry

If the world seems cold to you, kindle fires to warm it.

-Lucy Larcom

Oh Great Spirit, Divine One,

Embrace me in your love and light.
Guide me on my journey so I may grow and learn to
become a more radiant soul.

Give me strength and courage with roots dug deep so I
may be a beacon of light, peace and harmony.

Amen.

"There is magic in everything. Sometimes we just need to be willing to see it."

The world and Universe we live in is pure magic. There is magic all around us, and within us. The more we open our eyes to magic, the more we will see it and be able to tap into it.

The more we see it and tap into it, the deeper our spiritual connection and intuition become.

Affirmation:

My eyes are open to the magic around me.

Crystal & Essential Oil Suggestion: Spirit quartz & myrrh
Suggested Corresponding Chakra: Third eye and crown

JEALOUSY

Everyone feels jealous or envious from time to time. When we feel this way, it's usually because we feel there is something lacking within ourselves, that the other person possesses.

If we spend more time working on ourselves and building ourselves up, rather than being jealous of another, we will come to find that there's really nothing to be jealous or insecure of in the first place.

We all have unique qualities and we are all amazing in our own ways.

We also need to keep in mind that what we see on the surface is only one small part of the story. We don't know what the other person is going through on the inside or what it took for them to arrive at the place they are currently.

All the more reason to focus on our own qualities and lives. Because your qualities and life are fabulous.

Journal:

Where in your life do you feel insecure? What can you do to bring more confidence to the situation?

Dear God,

I ask you today to help me with healthy boundaries. I do not have to take on everyone else's pain and baggage. Likewise, I do not have to dump my pain and baggage on others. Help me to set a healthy boundary. I know that I can love others from afar without having to take on everything they're putting on me. I know that I can love myself and work through my issues without dumping them on others. Pease help to guide and support me through this.

Thank you.

Journal

Do you feel you acknowledge your true feelings? Do you express them? Why or why not? What would it feel like to fully acknowledge and express your feelings?

"By owning and expressing your magic, you inspire others to do the same."

The world needs more people embracing their magic and not being afraid to show it and share it.

When you own your inner magic and express this magic outwardly, you inspire others to do the same.

When we embody and express certain qualities, it helps give others the confidence to do the same.

And the world right now needs all of the confident magical goddesses we can get.

So step into that power, goddess. Own your magic and share it freely. Other goddesses are counting on you.

Affirmation:

I confidently share my magic with the world.

Spirit,

I really feel like I'm going to lose my freaking mind. I could really use a boost of patience. Please help me to tap into that calm and quiet space within. Please help me to remember to take a moment to breathe through this. I know that nothing lasts forever and this hectic tense feeling will pass.

Love, me.

Activity

THIRD EYE CHAKRA ACTIVATION

1. Get into a comfortable position in a space where you won't be disturbed.
2. Close your eyes and take some deep breaths while you visualize a beautiful purple or indigo light glowing in the center of your forehead.
3. See this light glowing brighter and brighter as it begins to spin. While the light is spinning, feel it clearing any stagnant energy.
4. Recite outloud, the seed sound aye (as in play) or the vowel sound u (as in uber)
5. Continue to chant and visualize for at least three minutes, or until you feel your third eye has been sufficiently activated.

Crystal & Essential Oil Suggestion: Labradorite & clary sage

Dearest Divine,

I am willing to look into my shadows. For I know that I can't have the light without the dark. While it's not always easy to look at the difficult things I may have pushed down, I know that I will be stronger and wiser by doing so.

Please help give me the strength and the guidance to embrace both the light and the dark within.

Amen.

Journal

What does it mean to you to "live your best life"? Do you currently feeling you're living your best life? Why or why not?

"Your past doesn't dictate your future. Learn from the past but don't let it consume you."

Whatever happened in your past, it's in the past. Some things from our pasts are very painful and hard to move away from, but we can either learn from our past or we can let it consume us.

Take whatever is upsetting or difficult from your past and use it to fuel you and make you stronger. You are not your past. But you can learn from it.

Honor your journey, the hard parts and the pleasant parts. If it wasn't for your unique journey, you wouldn't be the individual you are today.

Affirmation:

I celebrate my past and honor my journey.

Universe,

Thank you for working with me to manifest and bring into my life all that I desire and all that I dream of. For I know all that I can dream of and think of is already mine and that you are working with me to materialize this, or something better, into my physical reality.

And so it is

Journal
Where in your life have you given away your power?
Why did you let it go? Are you willing to take it back?

Suggested Corresponding Chakra: Solar plexus and root

"If you don't like the direction your life is headed, find a new path to travel."

At any point in our life, we can decide to take a different path. Just because you've set out on one particular journey or road, doesn't mean that you must stay on it until the end of time.

We are constantly growing and evolving, and consequently changing our minds. When this happens, it's okay to take a different direction.

It's especially okay to take a different path in life if you're currently on a path that isn't taking you in the best direction.

Sometimes it's difficult to find a new way to go, and sometimes we may have to leave familiar places or faces behind. But if finding a new path is of our highest good, then it's a necessary thing to do.

Affirmation:

I create my own journey.

Dearest Divine,

*I know that when I'm feeling insecure, I can turn my
attention to you.*
I am you and you are me.
I am Divine.
*Knowing that I am of Divine source energy reminds me
that I have nothing to be insecure about.*

I AM Divine.

Thank you.

Activity

SACRAL CHAKRA ACTIVATION

1. Get into a comfortable position in a space where you won't be disturbed. Take some deep breaths and close your eyes.
2. Imagine a warm orange light glowing in your pelvic region. See this light spinning and glowing brighter.
3. Feel this glowing spinning light as it clears out any stagnant energy that may be in your sacral chakra.
4. Say, out loud, the seed sound vam (pronounced vum) or the vowel sound ooo.
5. Continue to visualize and chant for three minutes, or until you feel your sacral chakra has been sufficiently activated.

Crystal & Essential Oil Suggestion: Unakite & Fennel

"The relationships in your life give you an opportunity for personal growth and healing."

Each person we come into contact with is a chance for us to grow or heal. The relationships in our lives are especially good for this.

Not all relationships are easy. I've found that the relationships in my life that are more difficult are the ones that have taught me a lot about myself and others.

This isn't to say that you should keep someone in your life simply to learn lessons from them. If a relationship is abusive or truly damaging in any way, remove that person from your life.

You don't need to have a person actively in your life in order to learn or grow from them. There are people in my life that haven't been active for many years, but I am still learning lessons and growing from my experiences with them.

Journal:

Are there any difficult relationships that you have had in your life? What did you learn from that experience?

It's your road, and yours alone. Others may walk it with you, but no one can walk it for you.

–Rumi

"Everything happens in divine timing, but that doesn't mean you get to sit on your ass and not work for what you want in life."

The Universe is working with us to manifest what we desire in life, and these things happen in divine time. But that doesn't mean that we get to desire something, announce it to the universe and then just sit around waiting for that desire to come knocking on our front door.

We must work *with* the Universe to create what we want in life. This means if what you're desiring is a new job, you must put in some effort. Fill out applications, turn in your resume and keep your eye out for job openings. The Universe matches our energy and our efforts. And it all happens in divine timing.

Trust that the Universe will open doors and bring the right things to you at the right time, while putting forth the effort on your end.

Affirmation:

I am working with the Universe to achieve my desires.

Beloved Universe,

I know that everything happens in divine timing. But sometimes it's hard to have patience. Please help me to tap into my inner peace while I await the wonder and beauty that is on its way to me.

Blessed be.

Activity

SMILE AT STRANGERS

I don't know about you, but I have a tendency to keep to myself when I go out on errands. While at the grocery store for example, I keep focused on what I need to be grabbing and don't pay attention to much else.

But something beautiful happens when we take a moment to connect with others. That persons eye you catch in the grocery store aisle? Instead of just looking away, give them a smile! They may or may not smile back, but the connection was still made.

When you smile at strangers, it brightens your day and it brightens theirs. It gives both of your heart chakras a little boost of light and love.

Next time you head out to run errands, try smiling at a few people you cross paths with. Make note of how it makes you feel.

Suggested Corresponding Chakra: Heart

"Sometimes we get to a point in our lives where it's more painful to stay where we are than it ever could be to change."

Sometimes we're aware that changes need to be made but we're too comfortable in the familiar. It may be painful and making you unhappy, but it's familiar nonetheless.

Eventually it becomes so painful that even the familiarity becomes too much to stand. That's when any fear of change flies out the window.

We get so sick of staying where we are, that we don't care how much work it will be to change or how scary a new path may be. We just know that we can't possibly stay where we are currently existing.

Affirmation:

Change comes easily to me.

Journal:

What is changing in your life that you may be having a hard time accepting? Why do you feel that is?

Suggested Corresponding Chakra: Root

Lord,

Thank you for making me a completely capable human being. Thank you for giving me the chance to take charge of my life and create with you, all that I desire. For I know if there is something I don't like in my life, I have the power to change it. With you by my side and within me, we can do anything.

Amen.

"We all have unique gifts and qualities. The world needs all different kinds of people, not copies of one another."

We are all made differently. With different ideas, dreams, aspirations, talents, personalities and skills. And not one is better than the other. Just different.

If all we had in the world were copies of one another, the world would be a pretty damn boring place. We need all sorts of people with all sorts of qualities and gifts in order to have a fully functioning and beautiful world.

What you're good at may not be what your friend is good at, or vice versa, and that's okay!

What you see as a quirk about yourself or something to not embrace, others see it as a gift. Embrace your unique qualities.

Journal:

What are three of your unique qualities? Do you freely express these qualities? Why or why not?

Affirmation:

I honor my unique gifts and I share them with the world.

Activity
RELEASING CEREMONY

You can do this ceremony any time you are wanting to release something from your life. This ceremony is especially potent during a full or waning moon.

1. Write down on a piece of paper something that you no longer wish to have in your life.
2. Light this piece of paper on fire and drop it into a fire safe bowl. You may choose to include an energy clearing herb such as sage, into the bowl.
3. As you watch the paper burn, envision and feel this energy leaving your life.
4. Once the paper is done burning, carefully dispose of the ashes.
5. Take out your journal and write down what you are wanting to bring *into* your life. You have released something from your life, therefore you now have energetic space available to bring in something positive and wonderful.

Please practice fire safety! Always have a fire extinguisher or water nearby.

Affirmation:

I release all that is not of my highest good.

Dear Lord,

Thank you for the difficult times. Thank you for not always making it easy for me. For I know that it's in these harder times that the big lessons are learned. I know that when times get tough, it's a chance for me to rise up stronger than before. It's a chance for me to step into greatness.

Amen.

"When working towards a goal, the more you enjoy the process, the easier it becomes to achieve that goal."

When we're working towards a goal or desire, it can be easy to get so focused on the end result, that we forget to enjoy the process. We forget to have *fun*.

When we have fun with our tasks or goals, it brings a higher vibration into what we're working towards, which makes the effort seem easier. It also seems to make the time go by faster. You know the old saying: Time flies when you're having fun!

Everything happens in divine timing, but that doesn't mean we can't have fun in the process.

Once we trust that everything happens in divine timing, and enjoy the process, the more smoothly things go and our goal is achieved more effortlessly.

Journal:

What is a goal you currently have? Do you feel like you're having fun in the process of achieving your goal? How could you make the experience more joyful?

Affirmation:

I trust in the divine process and have fun achieving my goals.

Dear God,

Sometimes I judge people. Please help me to see the love in others and the love within myself. Please help me to remember we are all one, and by judging others, I am only judging myself.

Amen.

Activity

CHAKRA LIGHT ACTIVATION

This is an activity I suggest you do each day, or at least once a week. It's a great way for you to stay up to date on the maintenance of your chakra system, while also checking in and seeing which chakras could use a little more TLC. I've found that the most convenient time to do this activity is first thing in the morning before I get out of bed, or last thing of the evening before I go to sleep.

1. Begin by envisioning a bright light above your head. This light is a loving light from source energy.
2. See and feel this light move down into the top of your as it lights up your crown chakra with a white light.
3. See and feel this loving source energy move down into each of your chakras, activating the chakra with its corresponding color of light as it passes through.
4. After this loving source energy has passed through your root chakra, envision the energy passing down your legs as it anchors into the earth.

Take note of how each of your chakras feel as the light is passing through them. Notice if any of the chakras felt particularly stiff, closed off or even very open.

Universe,

Thank you for all of the lessons you have taught me. Thank you for all of the blessings you have brought into my life. Thank you for your constant guidance and support.

Love, me.

THE CHAKRAS

If you're pregnant, nursing or have any health issues, please check with your healthcare professional before using essential oils.

Always check for any contraindications before using essential oils

ROOT CHAKRA

- Sanskrit word: Muladhara
- Kundalini (your spiritual life force) is located here
- Location: Base of your spine/tailbone
- This is your survival center and things relating to your finances, security, earthly matters, self-preservation, safety, grounding and physical self are located here.
- Color: Primarily red but also black, brown and gray can be used.

How can you tell if your root chakra is balanced?

- You feel secure and grounded
- You're able to easily relax
- You feel stable
- You feel physically healthy
- You're comfortable in your body and in your life

How can you tell if your root chakra is out of balance?

- You may feel fearful or anxious
- You may be quick to anger or act aggressively
- You might have a lack of discipline
- You may fear change
- You may be disorganized
- You might feel depressed
- You may be worried for your future and stressed about money and security

Physical symptoms that can be associated with a root chakra out of balance:

- Intestinal issues
- Being overweight or underweight
- Leg or back pain

- Immune system out of whack

Possible causes for a root chakra being out of balance:

- Having an unstable or difficult childhood
- Experiencing a lot of changes recently within your life
- Having money issues
- Not feeling safe in your environment

Essential oils for the root chakra:

- Frankincense: A very spiritual oil, frankincense helps to connect the root chakra to the crown chakra, creating alignment. It's a very grounding oil that helps you feel relaxed. ☐
- Vetiver: Grounds you in the present moment while helping you dig deep to deal with rooted issues.
- Patchouli: A wonderfully earthy oil, patchouli helps to keep you balanced and grounded.

Crystals for the root chakra:

- Red Jasper: Helps you with transitions and to manage a safe survival instinct.
- Smoky Quartz: Balances your survival instinct and can help you have a healthy relationship to money.
- Black Tourmaline: Balances root energies and grounds excess energy.
- Black Obsidian: Helps to balance past experiences so you feel safe in the present.

SACRAL CHAKRA

- Sanskrit word: Svadhisthana
- Color: Orange
- Location: About three inches below your belly button
- This chakra is all about your emotions, sexuality, sensuality, and creativity
- This chakra is the focus of your pleasures in life

How can you tell if your sacral chakra is balanced?

- You easily experience the pleasures of life
- You have healthy boundaries
- You can easily nurture yourself and others
- You have a healthy sexual appetite
- You're able to love and enjoy your body
- You're able to express yourself creatively and enjoy it
- You have a zest for life

How can you tell if your sacral chakra is out of balance?

- You may be addicted to pleasure or you will have a hard time finding pleasure
- You may be either extremely emotional or emotionless
- You may exhibit poor social skills and boundaries
- You might have a hard time expressing yourself creatively
- You could have a hard time "letting go" and enjoying life
- You may have unhealthy emotional attachments
- Could feel like you don't fit in
- You could have a difficult time being silly and embracing your childlike side

Physical symptoms that can be associated with an out of balance sacral chakra:

- Irregular menstruation or even ovarian cysts, endometriosis, or other reproductive issues
- Bladder or kidney issues
- Low back or hip pain

Possible causes for a sacral chakra being out of balance:

- Over indulging on things you want
- Being in an emotionally unbalanced relationship
- Being ridiculed socially (or bullied)
- Feeling neglected (currently or as a child)
- Not expressing yourself
- Feeling shamed, especially sexually or creatively

Essential oils for the sacral chakra:

- Wild Orange: This is an excellent oil at lifting your mood and bringing you joy. This oil is also good at boosting your creativity.
- Grapefruit: This oil can help you feel love for your physical body, which in turn can help you embrace your sexuality and increase your confidence.
- Cassia: Helps you embrace your silly side and not worry about looking life a goofball.
- Cardamom: This is a good oil if you're feeling very emotional. It can help you see things rationally. It also helps with self-control.

Crystals for the sacral chakra:

- Orange Calcite: Gives you willpower, can aid in creativity and can help increase your energy.
- Carnelian: Helps increase your energy levels, increases your personal power and helps boost your creativity.
- Unakite: Helps you figure out the root issue within this chakra.

SOLAR PLEXUS CHAKRA

- Sanskrit name: Manipura
- Color: Yellow
- Location: About two inches above your belly button.
- Governs your willpower, confidence, self-esteem, energy level, and how you see yourself

How can you tell if your solar plexus chakra is balanced?

- You are responsible and reliable
- You radiate warmth and love
- You have strong willpower
- You will embrace and embody your authentic self
- You're confident
- You feel energetic
- You're assertive

How can you tell if your solar plexus chakra is out of balance?

- You may experience low energy or extreme energy
- You may behave aggressively
- You may be judgmental to yourself and others
- You might worry a lot about what others think of you
- You could be manipulative
- You might feel like your authentic self isn't good enough
- You may feel you're not good enough
- You make need constant approval from others

Physical symptoms that can be associated with an out of balance solar plexus chakra:

- Diabetes
- Constipation
- Bowel issues

Possible causes for a solar plexus chakra to be out of balance:

- Physical, mental, emotional abuse
- Being shamed and ridiculed
- Feeling as if you've failed at lots of things
- You've let someone control or manipulate you

Essential oils for the solar plexus chakra:

- Lemon: Extremely uplifting and puts you in an excellent mood, raising your energy and your confidence. Be careful to avoid the sun for 12 hours after applying lemon (or any citrus oils) to the skin as it produces photo-sensitivity.
- Roman Chamomile: Helps to balance your emotions and helps to release any energy blockages within this chakra.
- Rosemary: Helps to ignite your inner fire, emotionally speaking. Physically, it can be helpful for digestive issues. Emotionally it helps you find your inner strength.

Crystals for the solar plexus chakra:

- Citrine: Helps to raise your confidence and self-esteem while motivating you to embrace your individuality
- Pyrite: Increases your confidence and helps you step into a leadership role

HEART CHAKRA

- Sanscrit name: Anahata
- Color: Green and pink
- Location: Center of your chest
- The heart chakra is all about compassion, love (for self and others), kindness, forgiveness and connection.

How can you tell if your heart chakra is balanced?

- You are compassionate
- You feel peaceful
- You are loving to others and yourself
- You are able to express empathy
- You're able to forgive
- You feel worthy

How can you tell if your heart chakra is out of balance?

- You might be antisocial
- You could be clingy
- You might be demanding
- You may be very critical
- You might feel lonely
- Self-love may be an issue for you
- You may hold onto resentment and have a hard time forgiving

Physical symptoms that can be associated with an out of balance heart chakra:

- Circulation issues
- Discomfort in the chest area
- Breast issues

Possible causes for a heart chakra to be out of balance:

- You let yourself be taken advantage of
- Breakups or heartaches
- Grief, losing someone
- Being hurt as a child

Crystals for the heart chakra:

- Rose Quartz: This is the crystal of love and is pretty much the "go to" heart chakra crystal. It helps with self-

love and with loving others. It's a very calming and nurturing stone.
- Green Jade: Increases love and nurturing and is a protective stone. Helps at filtering out energies that could be blocking your heart chakra.
- Peridot: Helps you release guilt while opening and cleansing the heart chakra.
- Amazonite: A soothing stone which helps balance your yin and yang energies.

Essential oils for the heart chakra:

- Geranium: Promotes emotional wellness and feelings of love.
- Jasmine: Promotes feelings of love and romance.
- Rose: The ultimate love oil.

THROAT CHAKRA

- Sanscrit name: Visuddha
- Color: Blue
- Location: Throat
- This chakra is all about speaking your truth, expressing your thoughts, listening to others and communication

How can you tell if your throat chakra is balanced?

- You are a good listener
- You're able to easily express your thoughts
- You speak up for yourself and others
- You communicate effectively
- You speak with honesty

How can you tell if your throat chakra is out of balance?

- You may have a habit of "biting your tongue"
- You might talk excessively or not at all
- You could have a hard time expressing your feelings or thoughts
- You may gossip about others
- You may find that you interrupt others a lot
- You may not be a very good listener

Physical symptoms that can be associated with an out of balance throat chakra:

- Tightness or tension in your jaw or neck
- Sore throat and ear aches
- Raspy voice or losing your voice
- Getting canker sores or acne around your mouth

Possible causes for a throat chakra to be out of balance:

- Feeling like your voice isn't being heard
- Being silenced a lot as a child or as an adult
- Not speaking up when your feelings are hurt
- Being afraid to speak your truth

Essential oils for the throat chakra:

- Peppermint: Great for the respiratory system, it can help you express yourself more easily.
- Eucalyptus: Good for the respiratory system, it helps you feel free and able to speak your truth more easily.
- Cypress: Helps give you fresh energy to vocalize your thoughts.

Crystals for the throat chakra:

- Lapis Lazuli: Opens and balances your throat chakra to help you express yourself.

- Turquoise: Balances and gives you confidence to speak more openly.
- Blue Calcite: Helps you express yourself and to understand unspoken messages. Also good at helping you hear your spirit guides.
- Blue Apatite: Helps with public speaking.
- Sodalite: Helps with self-expression and speaking honestly.

THIRD EYE CHAKRA

- Sanscrit Name: Ajna
- Color: Indigo or purple
- Location: Forehead, in between the eyes
- This chakra is all about your intuition and imagination. Also governs your thoughts and concentration.

How can you tell if your third eye chakra is balanced?

- You'll have a good memory
- You're able to easily visualize things in your mind
- You can "See the bigger picture"
- You will be very intuitive & trust that intuition
- You'll have a good imagination
- You may have detailed dreams that you remember

How can you tell if your third eye chakra is out of balance?

- You may be close minded
- You might not have much of an imagination
- You may have a hard time trusting or tuning in to your intuition
- You could have a hard time concentrating

Physical symptoms that can be associated with an out of balance third eye chakra:

- Vision troubles
- Migraines and headaches
- Getting dizzy easily

Possible causes for a third eye chakra to be out of balance:

- Ignoring your intuition
- Witnessing traumatizing or upsetting things
- Not embracing your imagination

Essential oils for the third eye chakra:

- Thyme: Helps you focus on your intuition and the bigger picture.
- Sandalwood: Will help quiet the mind so you can hear your intuition more easily.
- Lavender: Can help increase your intuition and imagination.
- Rosemary: Helps you to mentally focus.
- Clary Sage: Helps you interpret the intuitive messages you receive.

Crystals for the third eye chakra:

- Labradorite: I personally always have some near me when doing readings. Stimulates intuition and psychic gifts while also shielding you from negative energy.
- Lepidolite: Opens and activates the third eye chakra while helping with concentration.
- Amethyst: Helps you to hear your inner voice. Also helps prevent nightmares.
- Lapis Lazuli: Opens the third eye and increases psychic ability.

CROWN CHAKRA

- Sanscrit Name: Sahasrana
- Location: Top of the head
- Color: Violet or white
- Crown chakra helps with your connection to your Higher Self, enlightenment, spiritual connection, connection to higher realms.

How can you tell if your crown chakra is balanced?

- You will be an open-minded person
- You'll feel spiritually connected
- You will feel connected to your Higher Self & Inner Goddess
- You are open to the possibilities of a higher power

How can you tell if your crown chakra is out of balance?

- You may be critical of spirituality or may be completely addicted to it
- You could feel out of it or "spacey"
- You might get easily confused
- You could find that your ego is dominant

Physical symptoms that can be associated with an out of balance crown chakra:

- Migraines
- Dizziness

Possible causes of the crown chakra being out of balance:

- Having religion forced on you
- If you've been criticized for your own spiritual beliefs

Essential oils for the crown chakra:

- Frankincense: This is an extremely spiritual oil, used in many cultures for many years. Helps to achieve a meditative state while connecting you spiritually.
- Sandalwood: This is another very spiritual oil. Helps to quiet your mind so you can be open to spiritual guidance and connection.
- Ylang Ylang: This is another oil that helps to quiet the mind to connect spiritually. It's a high vibrational oil which pairs nicely with the higher vibrations of the crown chakra.

Crystals for the crown chakra:

- Selenite: This is a very high vibrational stone. Helps to open the crown chakra and connect to the spiritual realms of angels and spirit guides. A word of advice, this stone is highly powerful. Especially if you're sensitive to crystal energies. It can end up opening your crown chakra too much and leave you feeling spacey and out of it. When working with selenite I suggest to also use a grounding stone such as black tourmaline.
- Amethyst: Calms your mind and aids in meditation. Can also activate and enhance psychic gifts.
- Clear Quartz: This crystal amplifies energies and provides a clearing or stagnant or stuck energies. Helps the crown chakra to function better.

ESSENTIAL OIL & CRYSTAL REFERENCES

This is by no means a complete list of oils and crystals, but it's a good place to get started.

ESSENTIAL OILS

Anger: ylang ylang, bergamot, lavender, orange

Aura Clearing: cedarwood, lemon, myrrh, lime, juniper berry

Compassion & Self-Love: jasmine, geranium, cedarwood

Concentration: rosemary, peppermint, cypress, ginger

Confidence: cedarwood, juniper berry, lemon, lime

Creativity: frankincense, clary sage, peppermint, orange

Crown Chakra: vetiver, myrrh, sandalwood, frankincense

Dreams & Sleep: lavender, chamomile, marjoram

Forgiveness: frankincense, geranium, lavender

Grief: grapefruit, lime, cypress, white fir, Siberian fir

Grounding: frankincense, patchouli, cedarwood, vetiver

Heart Chakra: marjoram, rose, neroli, geranium

Inner Goddess: jasmine, neroli, rose, sandalwood, myrrh

Meditation: spikenard, frankincense, myrrh, sandalwood, palo santo

Patience: patchouli, vetiver, Siberian fir

Prosperity: patchouli, frankincense, white fir

Release: geranium, cypress, ylang ylang

Root Chakra: myrrh, patchouli, vetiver, cypress

Sacral Chakra: cassia, orange, neroli

Sexual Energy: patchouli, jasmine, cassia

Solar Plexus Chakra: lemon, fennel, lemongrass

Spiritual Connection: myrrh, ylang ylang, sandalwood

Thankfulness: jasmine, ylang ylang, rose, bergamot, grapefruit, orange

Third Eye Chakra & Intuition: clary sage, lavender, rosemary,frankincense

Throat Chakra: spearmint, peppermint, basil

CRYSTALS

Anger: angelite, peridot, rose quartz

Aura Clearing: selenite, aura quartz, kyanite

Compassion & Self-Love: rose quartz, malachite, aquamarine

Concentration: fluorite, lapis lazuli, quartz

Confidence: sunstone, citrine, moonstone, carnelian

Creativity: bloodstone, fluorite, ametrine

Crown Chakra: selenite, clear quartz, howlite

Dreams: lepidolite, ametrine, quartz

Forgiveness: turquoise, rhodonite, apache tear

Grief: apache tear, smokey quartz, rose quartz

Grounding: Tibetan quartz, black tourmaline, smoky quartz

Heart Chakra: rose quartz, jade, aventurine

Inner Goddess: apatite, moonstone, garnet

Intuition: labradorite, azurite, kyanite

Meditation: amethyst, black tourmaline, labradorite

Patience: amber, dumortierite, kyanite

Prosperity: pyrite, green aventurine, tiger's eye

Release: smoky quartz, dalmation jasper, rose quartz

Root Chakra: red jasper, black obsidian, smoky quartz

Sacral Chakra: bloodstone, carnelian, orange calcite

Sexual Energy: moonstone, rhodonite, lapis lazuli, bloodstone

Sleep: amethyst, sodalite, selenite

Solar Plexus Chakra: citrine, yellow jasper, sunstone

Spiritual Connection: celestite, Herkimer diamond, apophyllite

Third Eye Chakra: amethyst, labradorite, shungite

Throat Chakra & Communication: blue lace agate, lapis lazuli, angelite

AFFIRMATIONS

In this section you will find an assortment of affirmations for various needs.

General Body:

I listen to my body.
I fuel my body with nutritious things.
I am in-tune with the messages my body is sending me.
Each day I choose to nourish my mind, body and soul.
My mind is sharp, my body is healthy, my spirit is strong.

Happiness:

There is something to smile about in every day.
By bringing joy into my life, I encourage joy in others.
I am deserving of happiness.
I welcome happiness into my life.
I allow myself to be happy now.

Crown Chakra:

I know that I am always surrounded by love and light, divinely protected.
I am at peace with all in my life.
Inner peace comes naturally to me.
I see the good in others and they see the good in me.

Third Eye Chakra:

I am an intuitive goddess.
Intuition comes easily to me.
I trust the intuitive guidance I receive.

Throat Chakra:

My feelings matter and I speak up when I feel hurt.
I communicate my desires and needs with love and confidence.
I listen well to others.

Heart Chakra:

I do all things from a place of love.
I take time each day to do something kind and loving for myself.
I take time each day to do something loving and kind for others.
I forgive anyone who has harmed me in the past, including myself.
I am a radiant beacon of love.
The more love I put out, the more love I receive.
I love and honor myself, deeply and completely.

Solar Plexus Chakra:

I have all of the qualities within me to be successful.
I am successful in all that I do.
I am a confident person, letting my light shine bright.
I am a strong and capable individual.
 I achieve whatever I set out to do.

Sacral Chakra:

I easily tap into my sensuality.
I embrace my feminine energy.
I honor the cycles of my body.
Creativity comes easily to me.

<u>Root Chakra:</u>

I am secure. I am safe.
I attract the best circumstances into my life.
I easily find solutions to the things in my life.
I love money and money loves me.

TAROT & ORACLE CARD SPREADS

Posting one of the tarot spreads on social media?
Use #TheGoddessLifeBook

ROOT CHAKRA SPREAD

- What issue from my past is causing my root chakra to be unbalanced?
- How can I best work through this old trauma?
- What should I be focusing on right now in regards to my root chakra?
- What can I do to balance my root chakra?
- What do I need to heal within myself to best benefit my root chakra?
- How can I have a better relationship with money?
- What can I do to feel more secure in my life?

SACRAL CHAKRA SPREAD

- How can I best express my passions?
- What can help me feel more alive?
- How can I tap into my sexuality?
- How can I best express myself creatively? □
- What can I do right now to help my sacral chakra?
- How can I nurture my inner child?
- What is currently affecting my sacral chakra?

SOLAR PLEXUS CHAKRA SPREAD

- How can I improve my reliability?
- What is blocking me from feeling confident?
- How can I best balance my overall energy?
- What can I work on help me radiate love and warmth?
- Where in my life am I being manipulated?
- What is my authentic-self telling me?
- How can I embrace my authentic-self more fully?
- Where could I stand to be more assertive?

HEART CHAKRA SPREAD

- What is causing my heart chakra to be out of balance?
- What can I focus on right now to best balance my heart chakra?
- How can I be more compassionate to others (or myself)?
- How can I connect more with others?
- What could I forgive myself for?
- What could I forgive others for?

THROAT CHAKRA SPREAD

- Why is my throat chakra out of balance?
- What can I do currently to help balance my throat chakra?
- How can I be a better listener?
- What is preventing me from speaking my truth?
- How can I best express my thoughts?

THIRD EYE CHAKRA SPREAD

- How can I improve my concentration?
- How can I tap into my intuition more easily?
- How can I encourage my imagination?
- What are my dreams telling me?
- What is contributing to my blocked intuition?
- How can I best balance my third eye chakra?

CROWN CHAKRA SPREAD

- How can I be more open minded?
- How can I better connect to Spirit
- How can I better connect to my Inner Goddess?
- What is currently affecting my crown chakra?
- What can I do to gain a broader sense of Spirit?

SELF-LOVE SPREAD

- How can I love myself more?
- How can I show myself more compassion?
- What area of myself is requiring the most love at this time?
- What act of self-love can I show myself at this time?

RELEASING SPREAD

- What is currently causing me the most issues in my life?
- What in my life am I ready to release?
- How can I release this?
- By releasing this, what positive thing will I be able to replace it with?

INTUITION SPREAD

- What is my intuition trying to tell me?
- How can I better embrace my intuition?
- How does intuition show up for me personally?

GOAL PLANNING

- What is my current goal?
- What energy is blocking me from this goal?
- What should I focus more on to achieve my goal?
- How can I best achieve this goal?

PROSPERITY

- What is my current mindset about money?
- What do I need to heal in my relationship with money?
- What could I focus on to generate more money into my life?
- What is currently blocking the flow of money into my life?

FORGIVENESS

- What is causing me this current pain?
- What is required of me to forgive?
- Why am I having a difficult time forgiving?
- What can I do to move towards forgiveness?
- By forgiving, what am I making room for in my heart?

BIRTHDAY

- What was my main lesson from my previous age?
- What lesson can I expect during this age?
- What birthday message does my younger self have for me?
- What birthday message does my Spiritual Team have for me?
- What is something I should focus on for this age?

INNER GODDESS

- How can I better connect with my inner goddess?
- What message does my inner goddess have for me?
- How can I express the positive qualities of my inner goddess within my own life?

MIND/BODY/SPIRIT

- What are the current energies or lessons involving my mind?
- What are the current energies or lessons involving my body?
- What are the current energies or lessons involving my spirit?

CHILD/ADULT/ELDER

- What message does childhood me have?
- What message does adult me have?
- What message does elder me have?

PAST/PRESENT/FUTURE

- What from my past is currently affecting me?
- How is this past energy affecting me presently?
- How will this affect my future?

Many blessings to you, sweet goddess.

THE GODDESS LIFE PODCAST

Helping women connect to their inner goddess while nurturing their divine feminine essence.

Learn both practical and magical ways to work with your mind, body and spirit.

Live your most divinely empowered life.

New episodes weekly on iTunes!

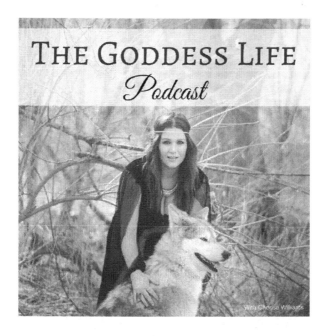

ABOUT THE AUTHOR

Cherise Williams is a wife and mama from Ohio. When she's not guiding others on their spiritual or holistic journey, she loves to spend her free time hiking, being with family, going to antique shops and investigating the paranormal.

Cherise holds several diplomas and certifications for spiritual and holistic studies.

www.CheriseWilliams.com
Instagram @CheriseWilliams.xo

Made in the USA
Columbia, SC
03 March 2021